THE FAT

Explains what fats are, the ~~~~~ types of fats,
their role in your diet and how you can keep fat intake
at a safe and healthy level.

THE
FAT
FACTOR

Everything _You_ Need to Know about Fats and _Your_ Health

JOHN O'MULLANE, Ph.D., & CAROL MUIR, Ph.D.

Illustrated by Mark Cripps

THORSONS PUBLISHING GROUP
Wellingborough, Northamptonshire

First published March 1986

© J. E. O'MULLANE and C. MUIR 1986

British Library Cataloguing in Publication Data

O'Mullane, J. E.
The fat factor: everything you need to know
about fats.
1. Fat 2. Diet
I. Title II. Muir, C.
613.2'8   RM 217

ISBN 0-7225-1184-1

Published by Thorsons Publishers Limited,
Wellingborough, Northamptonshire, NN8 2RQ, England.

Printed in Great Britain by
Richard Clay Limited, Bungay, Suffolk.

4 6 8 10 9 7 5 3

Contents

Introduction

Every cell in your body has been made from, and is maintained in a healthy state by, the food that you eat. This is often expressed in the saying 'you are what you eat'. On the face of it this appears to be a statement that hardly seems worth making because it is so obvious. The fact is that, even though most people are aware that what they eat may directly affect their health, few are actually well-enough informed to make the necessary changes to their diet.

Before you can tackle any problem, and particularly a diet-related problem, you need to be armed with the necessary background information that will allow you to make an informed decision. You might think that you are fairly knowledgeable about the role of fats in the diet. It is taken for granted that you understand the full implications of words such as polyunsaturated fatty acid and cholesterol. Or is it?

These words are often used in a pseudo-scientific manner to imply that if a product is high in polyunsaturates and low in cholesterol then it must be good for you. Advertisers often hit upon this ploy when it comes to devising an effective promotion. We recently saw an advert which said in bold letters 'At Last, Cholesterol-free Oil'. The advert went on to say that this oil was 'entirely free from cholesterol, high in polyunsaturates and rich in Vitamin E'. You would be forgiven for thinking that this was the first time that an oil had been refined with all of these properties. What the advert neglected to tell you was that virtually every vegetable oil contains such a small amount of cholesterol that it cannot be measured and that the most common vegetable oils, excluding olive oil, contain large quantities of polyunsaturated fatty acids. This company, and others like it, use such terms not necessarily for a straightforward description of the product but to link, in some way, the concept of good health and the composition of the oil. It is relying on the fact that you may only have a superficial knowledge of the role of fats in nutrition and that, in this case, 'cholesterol' is bad for you and 'polyunsaturates' are good for you.

In addition to this over-the-top style of promotion there is a general attempt by some newspapers to sensationalize scientific investigations and government reports. The lay person is left with the impression that 'all fats are bad for you' or the more general fallacy that 'everything nowadays is bad for you'. This is neatly summarized by a correspondent to *The Times* in June 1984 who writes:

The Times, 29.6.84, p. 9.   Talkback: The Food Scandal

I have been following the great food debate in your column with avid interest and would like to add this personal protest. I gave up smoking years ago for my health and my pocket, I have now given up drinking for medical reasons. My sex life is severely restricted because my husband is away from home most of the time, and, with four sons under the age of six, I don't have the energy for extra-curricular activities. If I now give up much of the food I enjoy, I might as well go and lie down under a passing truck.

But life need not be like this. We want to help you to appreciate the truth behind reports that you may come across by going back to basics, examining what the fats are actually doing in your diet, and seeing why they are important to life.

Firstly, we will examine the scientific background to fats, their chemical structure, properties and so on. You may think that this is unnecessary, but if you really want to understand the true facts about how fats work in the body you need to have a complete basic understanding of their composition. This will also help you when it comes to examining newspaper reports and advertisements critically. You might, for example, have heard about 'low-fat spreads' and that these are effective when used as part of a calorie-controlled diet. What is the difference between low-fat spreads and margarine or butter? How do polyunsaturated fats work? What does cholesterol do? These are all questions that will be dealt with.

Chapter 2 goes on to explain how fats are absorbed, distributed throughout the body, metabolized and excreted. It also examines the way in which fats are transported in the blood by the lipoproteins. We will then critically review the relationship between dietary fats and blood lipid diseases, such as atherosclerosis and coronary heart disease. You should be able to understand more about the major killers of our 'Western Civilization' after reading Chapter 3. Chapter 4 goes on to review some of the other influences on fat metabolism, for example, exercise, smoking and alcohol consumption.

In conclusion we suggest ways in which you might alter your diet to benefit from your new-found knowledge. You may find that your diet is perfectly suitable for you at the moment — so much to the good. But whatever the outcome we are sure that you will find out some revealing facts about yourself and your diet.

1

What Are Fats?

If you take a quick look around your kitchen, I would imagine that you would have very little difficulty in spotting the more obvious dietary fats. The packets of lard and butter are the more obvious *visible* fats in your diet. In the nutrition sense, however, this term includes the vegetable oils (such as corn oil) and animal oils (such as cod liver oil). They are all 'fats' in the way in which they are used by the body, although we usually only call something a 'fat' if it is solid at room temperature; it is called an 'oil' if it is liquid at room temperature. There is one general term that is used to cover both fats and oils and this is *lipid*. From now on, in this chapter, we will generally refer to fats and oils using the collective title of lipid.

Lipids As One Component of the Diet

If you are going to take positive steps to change your diet then you will need to know more about the composition of foods. As we mentioned above, the visible lipids are an obvious part of your diet and they can be recognized immediately by their characteristic properties. Lipids are, however, only one of three major constituents of your diet, the other two being carbohydrate and protein. The visible carbohydrates are substances such as sugar and starch, and the visible proteins are characterized by textured vegetable protein or other pure protein preparations.

Quite often, however, it is not always obvious from the outside what a foodstuff contains. We say that it has a *hidden* composition that can only be determined by chemical analysis. As a short test see if you can guess the hidden composition of the following foodstuffs: butter, low-fat spread, margarine, milk (whole), single cream, double cream, fatty beef, lamb and pork, lean beef, lamb and pork. Assume that each of them weighs 100 grams then try to estimate how many grams of this total are fat, protein or carbohydrate. If you think, for example, that milk contains 50 grams of fat then its percentage composition will be 50 per cent fat. If you think it is only 20 grams of fat then its percentage composition is 20 per cent fat, and so on. Remember that you want to consider fat, carbohydrate and protein and that there is also water in virtually all food.

Now check with Table 1.1 to see how good your knowledge of food composition really is.

Table 1.1. The percentage composition of some common foodstuffs.

Food	Lipid (fat)	Protein	Carbohydrate	Water
Butter	82	—	—	15
Low-fat spread	41	—	—	57
Margarine	81	—	—	16
Milk (whole)	4	3	4	88
Single cream	21	2	3	74
Double cream	48	2	2	47
Fatty Meat				
Beef	63	12	—	24
Lamb	72	6	—	21
Pork	72	7	—	21
Lean Meat				
Beef	5	20	—	74
Lamb	9	21	—	70
Pork	7	21	—	72

More of this type of analysis is presented in Chapter 5. It's not as easy as it looks is it? Now we will go through the table to extract the relevant information from the figures. The first thing you should notice is that, if you add up the percentage composition figures for a particular sample, you should obtain a total of 100 per cent. Take the figures for lean pork, for example, 7+21+72= 100 per cent. If you look at other samples, however, you find that this is not always the case and that some analyses add up to 97 to 99 per cent. The reason for this discrepancy is that each of the determinations is carried out separately and then the results are brought together and compiled for the table. There is an inevitable error introduced in this process, which leads to the small percentage 'going astray'.

Turning to the actual analyses, it may surprise you, if you were not already aware of it, that butter contains the same amount of lipid (give or take 1 per cent) as margarine. In effect this means that half a pound (225g) of butter has the same energy value, the same number of calories, as half a pound (225g) of margarine. How then can we make 'low-fat' margarines? On the basis of our table you can see that low-fat spreads contain only 41 per cent of fat compared with 82 per cent for butter or margarine. The answer to the question comes when you shift your eyes across to the column giving the percentage composition that is water. The manufacturers have greatly increased the water content of the low-fat spread from around 16 per cent to nearly 60 per cent by, for example, mixing in buttermilk. As the water content goes up, so the fat content, as a percentage of the total, comes down. This means, in effect, that you are paying for water *but* it does endow the product with other qualities, such as a greater ease of spreading, and gives it quite a different set of properties from the margarine or other starting material.

If you now look at the composition of lean and fatty meat you will see that the water content of lean meat is around 70 per cent, whereas the fatty meat has a water content of only 20 per cent. If you applied the same argument as before you might come to the conclusion that when you buy the lean meat you are actually buying more water. But you need to take into account the overall composition. The lean meat has a protein content of around 20 per cent, compared with the fatty meat value of around 8 per cent. The protein is that part which we normally regard as the flesh of the meat. Protein cannot exist in its natural state if it does not have a significant amount of water associated with it. If the water is taken out then the meat would become hard, brittle and virtually indigestible. The point we are trying to make here, then, is that you have to distinguish between the water that is added to a food simply to reduce its fat content, on paper, and the water that forms a natural part of the food.

While we are concentrating on the composition of various meats, you might have also noticed that the proportions of fat, carbohydrate and protein in each of the meats is virtually identical. What then makes beef different from lamb or lamb different from pork? The difference is the *type* of lipid, protein or carbohydrate from which the meat is constituted. Just as we use the term lipid to cover the fats and oils, so there is an even greater variability in the types of fats and oils themselves. Most people think they can tell margarine from butter (and maybe they can!) but on the basis of the figures given in Table 1.1 they would never be able to tell them apart.

So now we must examine the chemical and physical properties of lipids and find out what makes them different from one another.

The Structure and Function of Lipids

The most characteristic feature of lipids, which is obvious to anybody who has to wash greasy dishes, is that they do not dissolve well in water, even in hot water with washing-up liquid. This is an interesting observation, but it also has profound implications in what it tells us about the structure of lipids and the way that they are used by the body. Over 60 per cent of your body weight is water. All of the reactions that take place in the body are carried out in a water environment. It appears that lipids start off with a handicap in not being able to dissolve in water if they are to be effectively used by the body. The way that the body gets around this problem will be examined more fully when we have looked at their structure.

Lipids can be classified into four groups: fatty acids; triacylglycerols (triglycerides); polar lipids (phospholipids); and sterols. We shall now consider each of these groups in turn.

Fatty acids

The fatty acids are the basic building blocks of all of the classes of lipids. They are found in their own right in food but, more importantly, they are the functionally important part of the more complex lipids discussed later. In other words, they tend to govern the properties of the complex lipids to which they are joined.

Fatty acids consist of a number of carbon atoms in a single, unbranched chain, joined together by chemical bonds. Each of the carbon atoms has hydrogen atoms joined to it. A typical fatty acid is palmitic acid — see Figure 1.1.

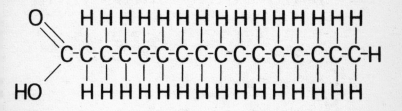

C is a carbon atom

H is a hydrogen atom

O is an oxygen atom

Figure 1.1 Palmitic acid.

Palmitic acid has 16 carbon atoms and another way of writing palmitic acid in shorthand would be C_{16-0}, which conveys a lot of information about the molecule that might not be obvious at first sight. The first subscript (16) denotes that it is a fatty acid that contains a total of sixteen carbon atoms. The second subscript (0) tells us that each of the carbon atoms are joined together by a single line, i.e. that they are joined together by single bonds. If the molecule only has single bonds between the carbon atoms then it also contains the maximum possible number of hydrogen atoms and it is referred to as a *saturated* fatty acid, which is commonly found in animal tissues.

There are also fatty acids that do not have only single bonds joining the carbon atoms together, e.g. oleic acid. See Figure 1.2.

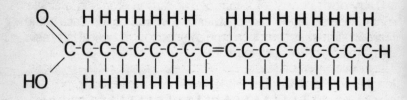

C is a carbon atom

H is a hydrogen atom

O is an oxygen atom

Figure 1.2   Oleic acid

What you should notice here is that halfway down the molecule there are two carbon atoms that are joined together by two lines; this represents a so-called double bond. Following on from the details given about palmitic acid you can see that the shorthand notation for oleic acid would be $C_{18:1}$. It has eighteen carbon atoms and one double bond. You will see that for each of the carbon atoms either side of the double bond a hydrogen atom is 'missing'. In this case we say that oleic acid is *unsaturated*. These type of fatty acids commonly occur in plant oils. Some fatty acids have more than one double bond, for example, linoleic acid ($C_{18:2}$), in which case it is said to be *polyunsaturated*.

So far we have mentioned one shorthand way of writing down the fatty acids. Sometimes we are more interested in comparing the function of the fatty acids in relation to structure and it would be inconvenient to have to write down the complete formula every time. There is a shorthand way of drawing the fatty acids molecule, leaving out both the carbon atoms and the hydrogen atoms. This is shown in Figure 1.3.

Figure 1.3 Shorthand representation of palmitic acid.

The most obvious difference between this notation and the previous longhand is that the line is 'kinky'. This is quite an important observation because it is how we imagine the fatty acid to be shaped in reality.

You may be wondering why we need to know all of this chemistry about the fatty acids. The reason is that the properties of the fatty acids — and consequently the effect they have in the body — are determined by: the *number* of carbon atoms joined together; and the *type* of bonds that join the carbon atoms together (either single or double and how many). Table 1.2 gives details of the melting points of some of the more common fatty acids.

Table 1.2 The melting points of some common fatty acids.

Name	Shorthand notation	No. of carbon atoms	No. of double bonds	Melting point (°C)
Palmitic	16:0	16	0	63
Stearic	18:0	18	0	69
Oleic	18:1	18	1	10
Linoleic	18:2	18	2	−5
γ-Linolenic	18:3	18	3	−11
Arachidonic	20:4	20	4	−50

As the fatty acid becomes more unsaturated (contains more double bonds) the melting point also comes down. Stearic acid is a solid at room temperature, whereas oleic acid is a liquid at room temperature. This is quite a dramatic change brought about by the presence of just one double bond.

To understand what is happening you need to appreciate the difference between a solid and a liquid. In a solid, the neighbouring molecules are packed closely together and there is a relatively strong attraction between the molecules because they can get so close together. In a liquid, the distance between the molecules is increased. Normally, you can heat a solid such as stearic acid and, if you look at Table 1.2, you will see that it will begin to melt at 69°C. At this point you have given the molecules enough energy so that they can pull apart and overcome the attraction between the neighbouring molecules.

If a substance is normally in the liquid state at room temperature

Figure 1.4

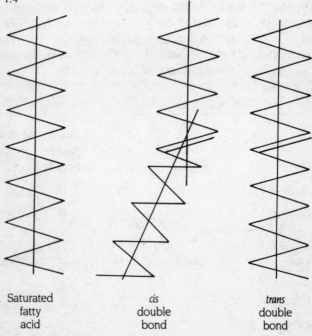

Saturated
fatty
acid

cis
double
bond

trans
double
bond

then, you can conclude, the attraction between the molecules must not be very great. There must be something about the molecule which is preventing adjacent molecules from packing very closely together.

Figure 1.4 shows the conformation (the shape that the molecule adopts) of a saturated fatty acid, one with a single (natural) *cis* double bond and one with a single *trans* double bond.

Oleic acid contains the natural *cis* double bond which, we can see, introduces an extra-large 'kink' into the chain. Obviously a collection of these molecules would not be able to pack as closely together as the saturated fat. The attraction between the molecules is lowered and the energy required to pull the molecules apart, and hence to cause the substance to melt, is less than for a saturated fat. Oleic acid and the other polyunsaturated fatty acids are most definitely liquid at room temperature, which reflects their increased unsaturated nature.

You will notice that a *trans* double bond does not introduce the same kinkiness as the *cis* double bond. The *trans* double bond does not occur in nature but may readily be produced in chemical processing. (*Trans* double bonds confer properties similar to those seen in saturated fatty acids.)

Essential fatty acids.

Some fatty acids, just like vitamins, are essential for normal growth and development. It was in 1753 that James Lind, a naval officer, made the first discovery of a link between diet and disease. He found that sailors on long sea voyages, deprived of fresh fruit and vegetables, developed a condition known as scurvy. He suggested that there was some ingredient of fresh fruit that prevented scurvy. We now know that this is vitamin C.

In a similar way that vitamins have to be supplied in the diet, there are certain fatty acids that are also essential because they cannot be made by the body. Two fatty acids, essential in a human diet, are linoleic acid and γ-linolenic acid; they are common constituents of plant lipids.

Triacylglycerol (neutral lipids)

This class of compound is sometimes referred to under the old name of triglyceride.

Even though you may not know it (because you may be unfamiliar with the name), you come across triacylglycerol every day. It is that visible fat which you use in cooking such as lard, vegetable oil and butter, and it is also that visible fat that gets deposited under the skin when you eat too much.

Many thousands of years ago, when man was a vigorous hunter, it was necessary to carry around a mobile energy store. A killing was made perhaps once a week (if you were lucky) and you would have had to rely on this food to carry you through to the next successful hunting period. The triacylglycerols make a very convenient store of energy in a fairly compact form. Other components of the diet can also be used to synthesize these lipids in the body. You will be only too aware that excess sugar, for example, can be converted to fat and stored underneath the skin. Neutral lipids are stored without water (the lipids 'refuse' it) although this is not true of, say, the main carbohydrate storage molecule, glycogen. It has been estimated that if we had to rely on glycogen, rather than lipids, an average man would weigh about 130kg instead of the present 70kg.

A major problem that we face nowadays is that we no longer have to hunt actively for our food but that we have still retained

the same sort of metabolism. This leads to problems such as obesity, which is a condition whereby the excess energy that is consumed is very readily transformed by the body into the storage molecule, triacylglycerol. This fat is stored under the skin and is all too obvious.

Chemically, the triacylglycerols consist of three fatty acids joined to a glycerol backbone. You may have come across glycerol before, it is that sweet colourless liquid that is popularly called 'glycerine'. Figure 1.5 shows the chemical structure of the triacylglycerols. It is precisely because each glycerol molecule has three fatty acids attached to it that the lipid is called a *tri*acylglycerol molecule.

The individual fatty acids occupying their place on the molecule do not have to be the same. With only three fatty acids the possible number of chemically-distinct molecules is twenty-seven. As it happens there are around ten fatty acids that are commonly found in foodstuffs, so it can be appreciated that there is potential for an enormous variability in the chemical structure of the triacylglycerols; this gives rise to the vast range of fats and oils that are available.

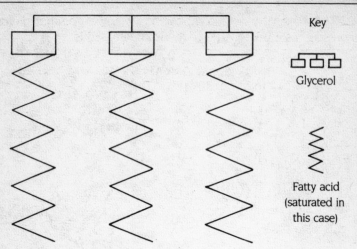

Figure 1.5   Triacylglycerol.

The properties of the triacylglycerol are determined by their constituent fatty acids. If the triacylglycerol contains a high proportion of saturated fatty acids then it will be a solid at room temperature. Conversely, the lipids with a high proportion of unsaturated and polyunsaturated fatty acids will be liquid at room temperature.

It is *not* true to say that lipids of animal origin are always saturated (solid) and that those of vegetable origin are unsaturated (liquid). It depends on the particular fatty acid composition of the fat, which in turn depends on the growing condition of the plant or the diet of the animal.

Table 1.3 gives an indication of the variability in fatty acid composition of some of the more common lipids. As before, the results are a compilation of a number of chemical estimations.

What is so surprising, at first glance, is that there are some large differences in the fatty acid composition of oils that you would otherwise think of as being very similar. Olive oil, for example, contains as little as 11 per cent linoleic acid whilst safflower oil contains 75 per cent linoleic acid. Conversely, olive oil contains 72 per cent oleic acid whilst safflower oil has only 13 per cent of

Table 1.3 The fatty acid composition of some common lipids expressed as a percentage of the total fatty acids.

Lipid	Palmitic 16:0	Stearic 18.0	Oleic 18:1	Linoleic 18:2	Linolenic 18:3	Arachidonic 20:4
Corn oil	14	2	30	50	2	—
Olive oil	12	2	72	11	1	—
Safflower oil	8	3	13	75	0	—
Soya oil	10	4	25	52	7	—
Sunflower oil	6	6	33	52	0	—
Coconut oil*	9	12	7	2	0	—
Lard	24	18	42	9	0	—
Cod liver oil	8	1	20	30	25	10
Herring oil	12	1	12	20	26	22

*Coconut oil contains over 60 per cent of shorter chain saturated fatty acids.

this acid. The really interesting part comes when you can appreciate how the different fatty acids are used by the body. We will come back to this when we look at the effect of fatty acids on cholesterol and the ramifications this has in the development of heart disease.

Animal fats, represented by lard in this table, contain a relatively high proportion of saturated fatty acids, and much less of the unsaturated and polyunsaturated fatty acids.

Fish oils are the one exception to the 'rule' that animal oils are mainly composed of saturated fatty acids. The two examples given in the table are typical of fish oils in containing predominantly mono-unsaturated and polyunsaturated fatty acids. Much attention has been focused on groups of people, for example Eskimos, who eat large quantities of fish oil. One particular piece of research has shown that the time that it takes for the blood to clot in this race is significantly longer than for races on a normal 'European diet'. This reduction in blood clotting times is believed to be beneficial in reducing the risk of developing heart disease. The particular fatty acids in the diet which are responsible for this effect are thought to be arachidonic acid and another polyunsaturated fatty acid found in very small amounts.

Polar lipids

This class of compounds is known under a variety of scientific names, the most commonly used being *phospholipid*, so used because all of these lipids contain phosphorus as part of the molecule (see Figure 1.6). We will refer to this class as the polar lipids because this term conveys more about how the molecule behaves in water.

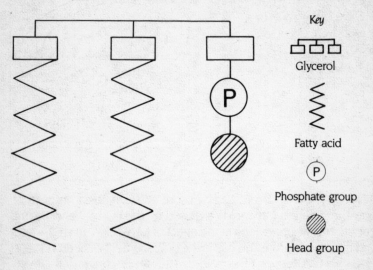

Figure 1.6   A phospholipid.

In this case we have two fatty acids joined to the glycerol backbone, instead of three as in the triacylglycerols. In place of the third fatty acid we now have an atom of phosphorus attached, followed by a so-called 'head group'. It is not important to remember the detailed structure so much as the effect that this arrangement has on the physical properties of the molecule. If you want to try to visualize the molecule, think of a matchstick. The head end that you use to strike the match can be regarded as the head group of the molecule. This head group has a completely different property to the 'stick' or fatty acids; it likes to be in very close contact with water. So within the molecule there are two opposite properties and you can imagine that there are a number of ways in which the molecules will prefer to arrange themselves when put into water (see Figure 1.7).

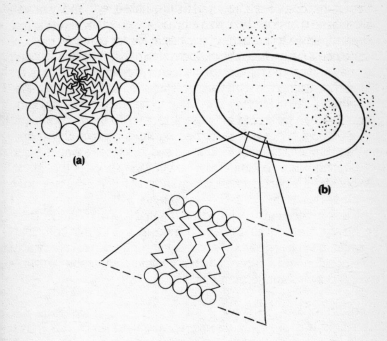

Figure 1.7 Polar lipids in water

In both of these cases, what the molecule is trying to do is reduce contact with water in the case of the part of the molecule that prefers to be out of water; in so doing, the head groups that prefer to be in a water environment are satisfied as well. The small balls of lipid, illustrated in Figure 1.7 (a), are very similar to the way in which lipids are transported around the body. In this case all of the sticks are pointing towards the centre of the particle and the heads are pointing towards the water.

The second illustration, Figure 1.7 (b), depicts another structure that is extremely important in relation to biological function. Around every cell in the body is a membrane that is composed mainly of polar lipids and cholesterol. On either side of the membrane there is a water environment. The arrangement of the phospholipids, as shown, produces an effective barrier around the cell. This membrane does not show up to the naked eye and you can appreciate, therefore, how these lipids are normally 'overlooked' when it comes to examining the tissue for fat content.

The phospholipids can be extracted from tissues (both plant and animal) and can be refined to produce a preparation that is fit for human consumption. One such preparation from soya beans is commonly called lecithin. If we were to be strict in the use of the term 'lecithin', we would only use it to refer to the phospholipid phosphatidylcholine (where the head group is choline). Quite often, in the commercial sense, lecithin is used to refer to a whole group of phospholipids. Lecithin from health food shops is thought to be beneficial in the treatment of a number of fat diseases (see page 78). Lecithin from soya beans contains a high proportion of polyunsaturated fatty acids and it is this that is of prime importance in the preparation. The fatty acid composition of lecithin from other sources, such as eggs, will have a significantly different fatty acid composition and will certainly not contain comparable amounts of the polyunsaturated fatty acid.

Cholesterol

This lipid was originally discovered in gallstones by the French chemist Fourcroy, about two hundred years ago. It is widely distributed in the body although it represents a fairly low proportion of the total lipid present. Its chemical structure is shown in Figure 1.8.

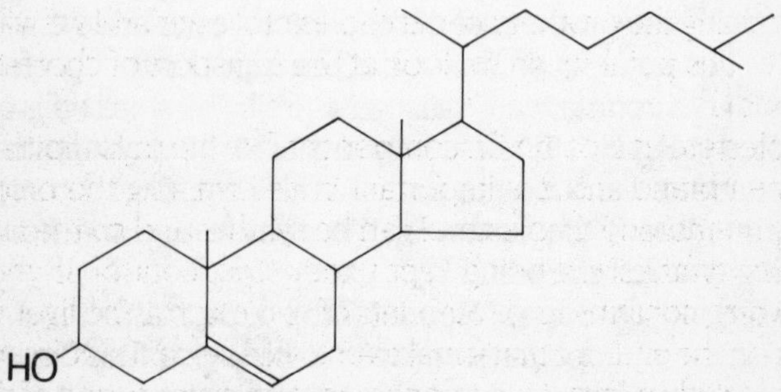

Figure 1.8 Cholesterol

As you can see, it is quite different in structure from the other lipids we have covered. It is a fairly bulky molecule and the fatty acids are nowhere in sight. You don't have to look far for them, however, because over 80 per cent of cholesterol exists in the form of cholesterol *ester*, i.e. the form in which a fatty acid is chemically joined on to the OH group of the cholesterol (Figure 1.9).

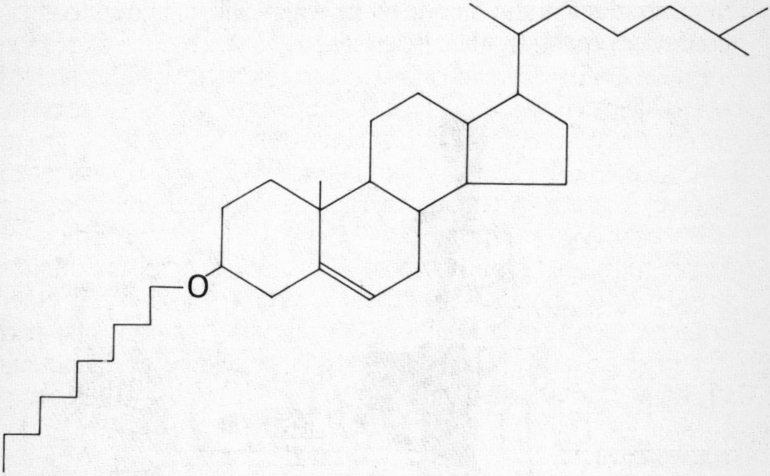

Figure 1.9 Cholesterol ester

Theoretically, any of the fatty acids could be joined to cholesterol in this way, although there seems to be some preference in the body over which ones are made. The fatty acid is important in determining the property of the cholesterol ester and we will come back to this point when we look at the transport of cholesterol in the body.

Cholesterol is a common component, like the polar lipids, of the cell membrane and it is important in determining the properties of the membrane. Cholesterol can be synthesized by the liver, the amount synthesized being kept under strict control. If you eat a diet which contains large amounts of cholesterol, the liver will cut down on the amount that *it* makes and vice versa. This observation is particularly relevant when it comes to an examination of the role of cholesterol in the development of heart disease. There is a hypothesis that the concentration of cholesterol in the blood is directly related to the risk of developing atherosclerosis. (Atherosclerosis will be considered in a later chapter but, briefly, it is a condition whereby the walls of the major blood vessels develop abnormalities, which consist of a high concentration of cholesterol esters and polar lipids.) The hypothesis states that high concentrations of cholesterol in the diet will lead to high concentrations in the bloodstream, which will in its turn lead to the development of atherosclerosis.

You might be forgiven for coming to the conclusion that cholesterol is always a 'baddie'. This is far from being correct. Cholesterol is required as a starting material for many of the essential bioactive molecules in the body (see Figure 1.10).

Vitamin D is sometimes called the 'sunshine vitamin' in recognition of the fact that it can be produced in the skin by the action of sunlight; it is also found in fish oils. The vitamin is required for normal development of bones and, if absent in the young, can lead to

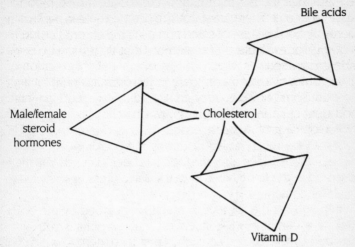

Figure 1.10

rickets, a disease which causes bowlegs. It is not normally required as a supplement to the diet; there are cases where giving too much vitamin D leads to bones becoming fragile.

The sex hormones progesterone and testosterone produce a wide range of effects in the body, either when produced naturally by the body or when given in medicinal preparations. The bile acids, starting from cholesterol, are produced by the liver and are secreted into the gut, where they help in the uptake of other lipids (see Chapter 2).

This concludes our examination of the structure and function of the particular lipid classes. Before the summary, we need to consider some general points about dietary fats.

Dietary Lipids

We have just looked at the lipid composition of foodstuffs and had a brief review of some of their chemical and physical properties. Armed with this information you might think that it is relatively straightforward to estimate the amount of fat present in a particular food and then use this information to calculate the overall intake of fat in your diet. There are still difficulties, however, in performing this calculation because of some complicating factors. Look at the following, for example, and remember that there may be others to be considered.

If you buy a piece of meat, how can you estimate its fat content? There are some obvious outward signs although there may be a good deal of fat in its hidden composition.

What oil or fat has been added to food during the cooking process? How much fat is lost during the cooking?

What fats are added after the food has been cooked? You might like to add butter to potatoes or to use salad dressings which have a high fat content.

When you eat the food, how much is absorbed by the body? There is a common misconception that everything you eat is absorbed by the body. The truth is that the extent to which you use the food depends as much on the type of person you are as to the type of food that you eat. If the food you eat passes quickly through the digestive system then you will not extract as much goodness from it than if it has moved more slowly. The pace at which food passes through your system might be influenced by your state of health as well as other 'normal factors'.

In general then, it seems that the role of fats is rather more complicated than it first appears. These factors are highlighted so that you can use them for your own information. It is good to be aware of them but do not let it dominate your thinking of the role of lipids in food.

Summary

Lipids (otherwise known as fats and oils) are a common and essential element of the diet. The properties of lipids are determined primarily by their fatty acid composition.

Saturated fats are mainly of animal origin and unsaturated fats are mainly of vegetable origin, but this is not a hard and fast rule.

Complex lipids are composed of fatty acids and another chemical structure. The properties of the complex lipid are determined by both parts of the molecule.

2

The Absorption and Metabolism of Fats

How are the fats that we have just examined in some detail able to get into the body and to exert their various effects? You will recall from the previous chapter that one of the characteristic features of lipids is that they do not dissolve in water. This presents a difficulty when it comes to the absorption and distribution of the lipids. The problem is that everything that takes place in the body, every reaction, occurs in a water environment. The two most important fluids in the body which are concerned with the transport of nutrients and the elimination of waste, the blood and the urine, only carry substances that dissolve in water. If a lipid is to be carried in the blood it has to be modified or combined with other molecules in such a way that its insolubility in water is no longer a problem. The whole process of digestion (the breaking down of complex molecules), absorption (the taking up of substances by the intestinal cells) and the transport (conveying the molecules to the site at which they are used) of lipids, is one that has evolved because of the unique physical properties of lipids.

The Digestive System

Figure 2.1 is provided as a revision aid of the human digestive system. This is basically a long tube whose prime function is to extract the maximum amount of nutrients from food and then to dispose of the waste. The diagram concentrates on the section to the small intestine, which is the region that we are most interested in.

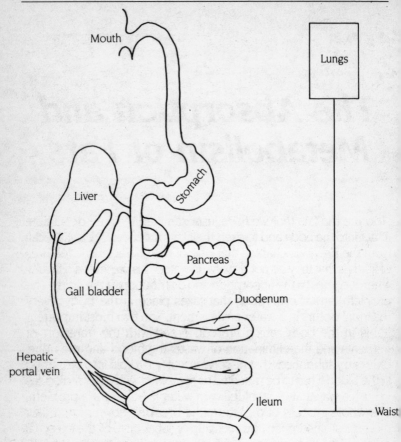

Figure 2.1   The digestive system

You should note the relative positions of the various parts and appreciate that this is a diagrammatic representation.

The mixture of foodstuffs, which should have been chewed forty times, is passed down to the acid bath of the stomach. The whole purpose of primary digestion is to break down the large molecules into smaller units that can be more easily taken up by the intestinal cells. There is some primary digestion of the proteins and carbohydrates in the stomach, but the lipids are left virtually untouched.

The churning action of the stomach does, however, help to form an emulsion of the lipids in water. The easiest way to try and visualize an emulsion is to think of the example of milk in a bottle. When the milk arrives on your doorstep there is an upper 'cream' layer which contains a high proportion of fat. When you shake the bottle of milk you are forming an emulsion of the 'fat' in the 'water' of the milk. When an emulsion is formed in the gut it is far easier for the lipid to be attacked by agents that will break it down into smaller pieces. This does not happen until the emulsion has passed from the stomach into the duodenum.

If you refer to Figure 2.1 you can see that the openings from the pancreas and the gall bladder are found in the duodenum. The pancreas releases a mix of enzymes and bicarbonate (which neutralizes the acid from the stomach). Enzymes are protein molecules that are specifically designed to chop up the carbohydrates, proteins and lipids. The lipids have their fatty acids chopped off and the two parts of the molecule are absorbed separately in this form.

The gall bladder releases bile which also helps in the absorption of the lipid. Bile is a green liquid which contains a mixture of fatty acids, neutral fats, phospholipids, cholesterol and, most importantly, bile salts. The bile salts and phospholipids help to form a better emulsion of the lipids and so aid their absorption. What actually happens is that the bile salts and phospholipids combine with the lipids to form rather large aggregates. The lipids are then attacked by the enzymes that specifically chop off the fatty acids. The fatty acids, and the other part of the fat molecule that is left, remain with the bile salts. The products of the digestion are rapidly absorbed by the cells lining the lower part of the intestine, so reducing the particle in size. The bile salts are not absorbed here. If you were able to look inside the intestinal cells during this process you would find that droplets of fat begin to form. This is because the fatty acids and glycerol that have been absorbed separately are now rejoined within the cell. As the lipid is insoluble in water, droplets are precipitated in the cell. From here the lipid is passed on to the lymphatic system and then distributed around the body by the bloodstream.

So what becomes of the bile salts? Most are actually absorbed further down the gut in the ileum. From the ileum they are passed on via the hepatic portal vein and thence to the liver. Here they are mixed with the bile salts that are synthesized by the liver and they pass out to the gall bladder where they are used again. The bile salts are, therefore, recycled, as shown in Figure 2.2, although some bile acids and salts are also excreted in the solid waste.

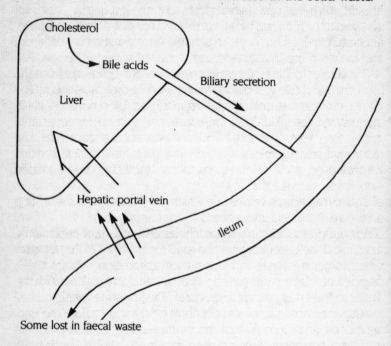

Figure 2.2

This recycling is referred to as the enterohepatic circulation.

Factors Affecting Absorption

So far we have talked as though all of the lipid that is present in the diet is absorbed. This is far from being correct. The amount of fat that is absorbed is related to the fats and to other substances in the diet. Research workers have always had a keen interest in finding out how much fat we absorb, in order to design more efficient diets or to obtain a better understanding of the process of digestion. Quite often the subjects for these trials are the inmates of prisons or are in hospital for ailments other than dietary-related disorders. A tube is inserted in the stomach and a mixture of fats is passed directly through this tube. Blood samples are taken at regular intervals and faecal samples are tested for their fat composition. From studies of this type it is possible to calculate accurately the extent to which a particular type of fat is absorbed and the influence that other dietary fats may have on the process.

The earliest results of such experiments showed that about 90 per cent of triacylglycerol-containing saturated fats was absorbed, compared with around 96 per cent of triacylglycerol-containing unsaturated fats. Although there is not a huge difference in the extent to which these two types are absorbed it does reflect a difference in the *manner* of absorption. It seems to indicate that the lipid that is 'liquid' at room temperature will be absorbed to a greater extent than the one that is more 'solid' at room temperature. The absolute differences between the saturated and unsaturated fatty acids are, however, quite small.

A more dramatic effect is seen in the absorption of cholesterol from the diet. It is quite usual for anything from 20 to 50 per cent of the total cholesterol to be absorbed. In other words, up to 80 per cent of the cholesterol can pass through the gut without being absorbed. As you can imagine, there is a great deal of interest in reducing the absorption of cholesterol from the diet. If we can find ways of preventing cholesterol from being taken up by the gut, then it will be one way of reducing the subsequent level of cholesterol in the blood.

The absorption of cholesterol depends on the amount and type of other fats in the diet. We did some research recently which showed that the absorption of cholesterol is less when given with dietary phospholipids (e.g. lecithin) than when it was given with an equivalent amount of corn oil. The results suggest that one way of reducing the absorption of cholesterol is by increasing the amount of phospholipid in the diet. In practice you may not be able to do this and it is probably better to try and reduce your total intake of cholesterol, rather than trying to block the excess.

Distribution of Lipids

So far we have looked at the ways in which fats are absorbed and we have indicated that once they are taken into the cells lining the intestine, they are put back together again. From here the lipids have to be passed on to the bloodstream. The blood is the major transport medium in the body. Just as motorways and trunk roads link the various parts of the country so the arteries and smaller blood vessels transport materials to all parts of the body. The blood perfuses all of the organs, the most important (as far as we are concerned) being the liver. Having been absorbed from the intestine, most of the lipids pass directly to the liver; to be absolutely precise some lipids come via the hepatic portal vein, although most lipids enter the bloodstream via the thoracic duct, a lymphatic vessel. The liver acts like the warehousing facilities at the docks, it takes in the nutrients and then controls the levels of these nutrients in the bloodstream.

Lipids in Blood

In general, we are not concerned with the way in which lipids end up in the blood but with what they do when they get there. We are, therefore, going to miss out the step between absorption of lipids by the intestine and the form in which they are carried in the blood.

We have emphasized before that lipids are insoluble in water and that, in order for them to be transported in blood, there must be some 'modification' of the lipid. The way in which lipids are 'dissolved' in blood is by associating them with proteins, which are generally very soluble in water. If you take a sample of blood you would find that the bulk of the lipid is loosely associated with proteins to form complexes known as *lipoproteins*. The attachment of the protein to the lipid is not permanent, but it is a convenient means by which the lipid can be transported from place to place.

The proportion of lipid to protein is quite variable. As the proportion of protein in the particle increases so the weight per volume — the density — of the particle increases. In biology there is a tendency to observe and classify. It is not unexpected then

to find that the lipoproteins are classified according to their relative densities.

One way of examining a blood sample would be to extract the red blood cells and allow the liquid part of the blood to stand in a corner for a few days. If you did this you would find that the lipoproteins in the blood would begin to separate out according to their relative densities. The same thing happens to, for instance, a bottle of wine that has had the sediment disturbed. It takes time for the wine to clear again. If you watch the progress of the clearing you would find that it was a gradual process from the top and the 'heaviest' — in fact the densest — particles would separate out first. A much quicker way of doing this is by putting the tube in a machine called a centrifuge. This spins the tube, which exerts a force on the suspended particles and causes them to separate out very quickly. Using this method it is possible to obtain rapidly a quantitative estimation of the lipoprotein composition of the blood.

Figure 2.3 illustrates the lipoprotein composition of blood. The range of the density bands were chosen to reflect accurately the properties of the particles within the band, and their names correspond to their density, i.e. Very Low Density Lipoprotein (VLDL), Low Density Lipoprotein (LDL) and High Density Lipoprotein (HDL).

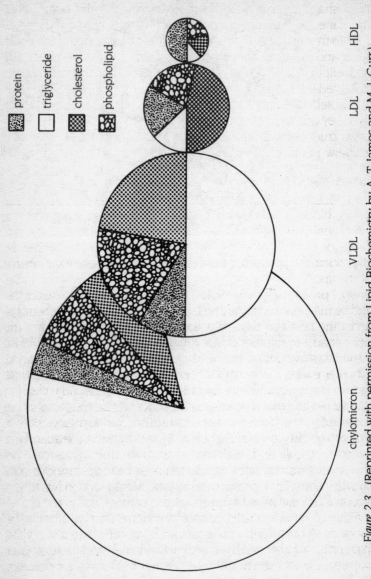

protein

triglyceride

cholesterol

phospholipid

chylomicron   VLDL   LDL   HDL

Figure 2.3 (Reprinted with permission from Lipid Biochemistry by A. T. James and M. I. Gurr.)

Their shape is reminiscent of the way in which the polar lipids spontaneously arrange themselves in water (Figure 1.7 (a), page 25). On the surface of the particles are the head groups of the polar lipids and proteins that can come in contact with water, the part of the lipid that is 'water hating' is on the inside. The particles are stabilized by the mutual interaction of lipid and protein. When the lipoproteins are drawn as in Figure 2.3 there is a tendency to think that they are separate entities that never change. This is far from being true. There is a constant flux in the lipoproteins which we will now go on to consider.

Chylomicrons

If your blood is taken say half an hour *after* a meal, it would be a good deal cloudier than a sample taken *before* the meal. The main cause of this cloudiness is the presence of a large number of chylomicrons. You can see from Figure 2.3 that these are the largest of the lipoproteins and consist of a core of triacylglycerol and a coat of protein and polar lipid on the surface. The chylomicrons are the main transport particles of the triacylglycerol and are taken up by the liver and adipose tissue. (Note: We tend to think of fat cells, or adipose tissue, as being an inert storage depot but in fact they have a high rate of metabolism and can be readily influenced by other events in the whole body. Adipose tissue can be used to build up triacylglycerol and to break it down again.)

When a chylomicron comes into contact with adipose tissue an enzyme on the surface of the fat cells breaks down the triacylglycerol to give free fatty acids and glycerol. These products are absorbed by the fat cell and built up again into triacylglycerol. The chylomicrons are thereby rapidly removed from the bloodstream and the excess lipid stored in the adipose tissue. One to two hours after a meal the blood appears 'clear' again.

Although chylomicrons contain a relatively small amount of cholesterol, the amount of cholesterol present in them is critical in determining how much the body will actually produce itself. You will be aware from the previous chapter that the liver makes cholesterol in the body. The amount of cholesterol that is made in the liver is controlled by the amount of cholesterol released from the chylomicrons. This is not entirely surprising when you consider that chylomicrons are a fairly good indicator of the lipids in the diet. It makes sense for the liver to cut down on the amount *it* is making if a lot is being absorbed from the diet.

Very Low Density Lipoproteins (VLDL)

These particles contain a high proportion of triacylglycerol, which is thought to be taken up by adipose tissue in a similar way to the triacylglycerol in chylomicrons.

Low Density Lipoproteins (LDL)

These lipoproteins are synthesized in the liver and are the major carrier of cholesterol in the blood. If you refer to Figure 2.2 (page 34) you can see that LDL contains a greater proportion of cholesterol than any of the other lipoproteins. When a biochemist measures the concentration of cholesterol in the blood he is in effect measuring the cholesterol in LDL. Because of its role in the carriage of cholesterol, LDL has had more than its fair share of attention.

Cells require cholesterol for normal growth and development. The way in which the cells recognize LDL is by having specific areas on the surface of the cell that are receptive to the protein in the LDL. These areas contain so-called 'receptor' molecules that can specifically recognize the protein part of the LDL.

Once the LDL has been trapped by the outside of the cell it is able to take in the lipoprotein and digest it within the cell. In summary then, cholesterol is carried mainly as Low Density Lipoprotein and is taken up specifically by cells after combining with a receptor on the cell surface.

So far we have just covered the normal case, where the concentration of cholesterol in the blood is a reflection of the cholesterol and the fatty acid composition of the diet. There is a case, however, where individuals have a very high level of cholesterol in the blood that is not related to high intake of cholesterol. This is a genetically inherited condition known as familial hypercholesterolaemia. It has been found that these individuals do not have a normal LDL receptor molecule on the surface of their cells. As the cholesterol cannot be taken into the cell, the concentration of cholesterol in the blood is four to six times that of the normal individual. As a consequence of an increased concentration of cholesterol in the blood there is an increased risk of the cholesterol forming deposits in the blood vessels. This information has been used to suggest that increased levels of cholesterol in the blood of normal individuals may lead to lipids being deposited in their blood vessels. This is covered in more detail in the next chapter.

High Density Lipoprotein (HDL)

These are the smallest of the lipoproteins and are believed to arise in the blood due to modification of VLDL. HDL consists of a spherical particle which has a central core of cholesterol esters and hydrocarbon chains of phospholipids, surrounded by a surface coat containing the polar heads of phospholipids and the proteins (see Figure 2.4).

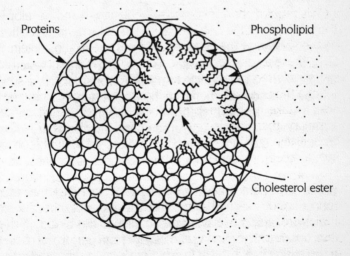

Figure 2.4   High Density Lipoprotein.

The cholesterol esters appear to play a vital role in the structure and function of the HDL particle. How do these cholesterol esters come about? The HDL particle is thought to start off life with very little cholesterol ester and it adopts a disc shape. As the HDL passes around the blood it acts like a scavenger in that it picks up cholesterol from tissues and converts this cholesterol to cholesterol ester. The enzyme that is responsible (in the blood) is called lecithin cholesterol acyl transferase — or LCAT for short. The enzyme works by chopping off a fatty acid from phosphatidylcholine (lecithin) and attaching it to cholesterol.

i.e. Cholesterol + Lecithin $\xrightarrow{\text{LCAT}}$ Cholesterol + Lysolecithin
                                                              ester

The cholesterol ester so formed prefers to be on the inside of the particle — away from the water. As more and more cholesterol esters are formed, so the particle transforms from a disc to a sphere. It can be appreciated, therefore, how cholesterol can be removed from the tissues and taken on board the particle.

This is why we think polyunsaturated fatty acids are important in reducing the concentration of cholesterol in the bloodstream. If the cholesterol ester that is formed contains an unsaturated fat then more of the cholesterol ester molecules can be stored in the centre of the particle and it grows in size. When HDL is then excreted, more of the cholesterol is removed. This also explains the potentially beneficial effects of having raised HDL in the blood, in that it is concerned with removing cholesterol from peripheral tissues and transporting it to the liver from where it can be excreted in the bile.

Summary

Lipids are formed into an emulsion in the gut and taken up by the cells lining the intestine. The lipids are, themselves, insoluble in blood but are combined with proteins to form particles known as the lipoproteins.

The major classes are HDL (High Density Lipoprotein) and LDL (Low Density Lipoprotein). LDL transports cholesterol to the tissues of the body and HDL transports cholesterol away from the tissues.

3

Diseases of Fat Metabolism

In the previous chapters we have examined how fats are a normal part of our diet and the way in which they are used by the body. We have tended to concentrate on the background aspects of fat nutrition simply because this part of the story is often neglected, even though it is very interesting. We will now turn to those aspects where the control systems of fat metabolism may be corrupted. This may be of our own doing by, for instance, an excessive intake of 'harmful fats' in the diet, or it may be a response of the body over which we have no control. Either way, by understanding fat-related diseases it should be possible to mitigate the impact that the disease state has on the body.

Disturbances in lipid metabolism are often closely associated with the so-called 'Western diseases', a term that was coined to suggest that these are diseases of affluent societies where the over-consumption of fats is a major factor. Most people would readily accept that heart disease is important here, although we will also consider obesity, diabetes, gallstones and certain forms of cancer.

Atherosclerosis and Coronary Heart Disease

Every year in Britain coronary heart disease kills more than 35,000 men before retiring age. It is statistically the largest killer in our country and accounts for nearly a half of the men who die in middle age; and recently women are being affected to a greater extent than ever before (see Figure 3.1). A depressing thought is that Britain (in particular Scotland and Northern Ireland) has the highest rate of deaths from heart disease compared with other countries that have had big drives to stem this epidemic — and with some success

— notably the United States, Canada, New Zealand, Finland and Belgium. In Britain the death rate is only just beginning to subside and an increased effort is being made at the national level to encourage this trend.

Achievement of a real reduction in deaths from coronary heart disease can only be made if a fuller understanding of the disease process is brought to the public's attention. This is what we set out to show here.

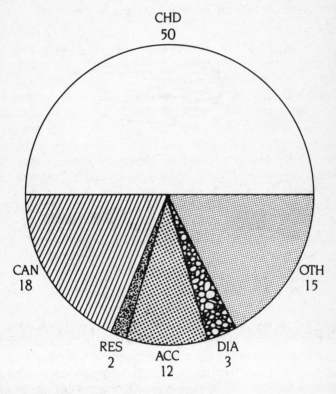

Key
CHD: coronary heart disease, CAN: cancer,
RES: respiratory diseases, ACC: accidents,
DIA: diabetes, OTH: others

Figure 3.1 Death rates in Britain

What is Atherosclerosis and Heart Disease?

Atherosclerosis is the scientific name given to the process whereby blood vessels become narrower due to the deposition of lipids and other substances. The vessels can be thought of as being similar to the pipes of a central heating system. As a central heating system gets older the pipes tend to get narrower due to the 'furring up' with salts that are normally dissolved in the water. In a similar way the pipes of the blood system may get 'furred up' with lipids and other materials that are normally present in the blood.

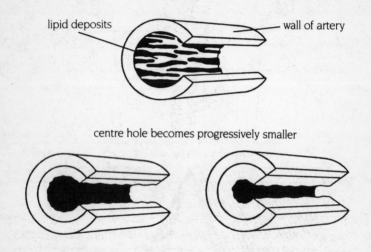

Figure 3.2 Narrowing of an artery: Atherosclerosis

Figure 3.2 shows diagrammatically how this process leads to a reduction in the size of the hole through which the blood can travel. As the size of the hole becomes narrower the heart has to work harder to circulate the blood. This in itself can lead to health problems such as angina. A person suffering this condition finds exercise difficult, although life is otherwise normal. Angina can be well treated with medication.

Coronary heart disease will not necessarily be associated with conditions such as angina, but the underlying causes are similar. The heart is simply a large muscle that acts like a pump to supply blood to all of the other body organs and tissues. The heart *itself* requires a supply of blood to remain active. This blood to the heart muscle is supplied by the coronary arteries as shown in Figure 3.3.

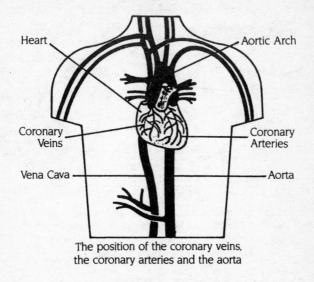

The position of the coronary veins, the coronary arteries and the aorta

Figure 3.3   The blood supply of the heart

The process of atherosclerosis can also lead to a narrowing of these coronary arteries. As they are smaller than the major blood vessels it is possible that their narrowing will cause the heart more problems than if the narrowing were to occur in a larger vessel.

An advanced state of the disease will involve deposits of calcium, which will decrease the elastic properties of the artery and will make the circulation even less efficient. Once the artery has been narrowed by this process then a clot (otherwise known as a thrombus) can adhere to the injured vessel wall and cause a blockage of the artery. If this occurs in one of the coronary arteries then the blood supply to the heart muscle can be cut off. When this happens, a part of the heart muscle is deprived of blood, stops functioning and dies. This is called a heart attack, which in some people is fatal but in others recovery may be accompanied by little or no disability.

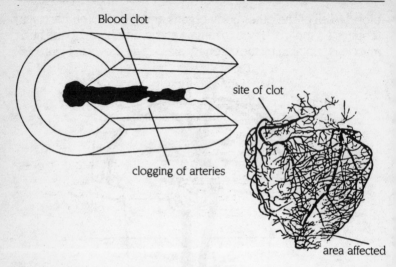

How a blood clot in a main coronary artery can starve a whole area of heart muscle of blood and produce a heart attack

Figure 3.4   The effect of a heart attack

Risk Factors

In spite of much research the precise underlying causes of coronary heart disease have not been discovered. An examination of the general public over the past twenty to thirty years has established a link between the symptoms of the disease and various factors which might cause the disease. These findings are called risk factors and it is generally accepted that there is no single cause (or risk factor) of heart disease, but that there are many which include those listed opposite.

This book is mainly concerned with fats and so here we will only concentrate on those risk factors closely associated with fat.

Fat in Atherosclerosis

Atherosclerosis is basically an accumulation of fats, particularly cholesterol and its esters, within the arterial wall. The fats are derived directly from the fat in the blood or by synthesis of fat within the

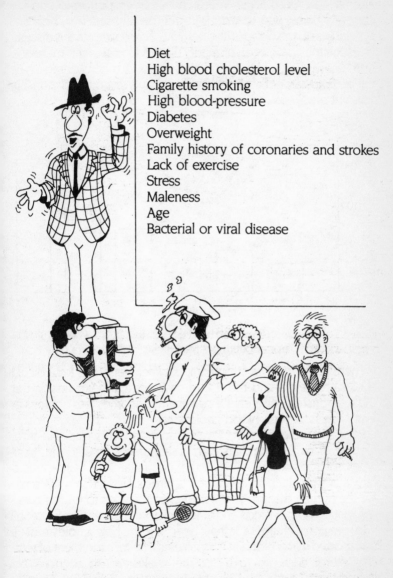

Diet
High blood cholesterol level
Cigarette smoking
High blood-pressure
Diabetes
Overweight
Family history of coronaries and strokes
Lack of exercise
Stress
Maleness
Age
Bacterial or viral disease

arterial wall itself. Much research has been performed and is currently under way to work out the mechanisms by which this occurs. Due to the obvious involvement of cholesterol in this disease, investigations have been primarily directed towards this molecule. In the early 1970s high blood cholesterol was considered to be the best indicator of atherosclerosis, although a strong relationship was not always found (Figure 3.5).

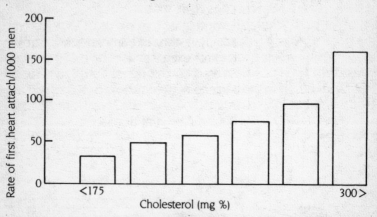

Figure 3.5 Cholesterol levels and heart disease. (Reprinted with permission from Boehringer Mannheim GmbH.)

There is obviously a strong link between very high total blood cholesterol levels and the risk of developing a heart attack, but the relationship between the two events becomes less obvious at lower levels of total blood cholesterol.

Raised blood cholesterol levels in animals, either by cholesterol feeding or by feeding diets high in saturated fatty acids, induces atherosclerosis, whereas diets with predominantly polyunsaturated fatty acids produce far less atherosclerosis. Using this knowledge for the human disease you would expect always to have a close association of cholesterol and atherosclerosis. But why is this not so?

In previous chapters it has been shown how cholesterol is transported in the blood in lipoproteins. The measurement of total cholesterol adds up to all of the cholesterol in each of the lipoproteins, i.e. in Low Density Lipoprotein (LDL), High Density Lipoprotein (HDL) and so on. The function of LDL is to transport cholesterol to the cells of the body, whereas HDL tends to take up cholesterol from the tissues. In simple terms then, an increase in LDL-cholesterol can be seen as speeding up the atherosclerosis process by making more cholesterol available and HDL-cholesterol will tend to have the opposite effect. In order to appreciate fully what might be happening an estimation has to be made not only of the *total* cholesterol present in the lipoproteins but also whether it is contained within LDL or HDL.

Recent studies have shown that high levels of HDL-cholesterol are good for you. It indicates that the cholesterol is being carried around in a form that will not be deposited in the blood vessels, whereas a high LDL-cholesterol promotes deposition of cholesterol in the arteries. It is the balance between these two lipoproteins that is important in predicting the risk of coronary heart disease.

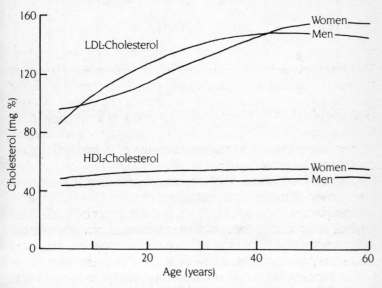

Figure 3.6   Cholesterol levels and age

It can be seen from Figure 3.6 that HDL-cholesterol levels increase with age in men after puberty but a slight increase in women has been reported until menopause. LDL-cholesterol, on the other hand, does increase with age in both men and women. Here, men have a higher LDL-cholesterol level than women until menopause, when women overtake the men. Also at this age there is no further increase in LDL-cholesterol in either men or women.

High LDL-cholesterol levels are associated with an increased risk of heart disease and it is important to distinguish between the two lipoproteins when a raised cholesterol level is reported. In Table 3.1 are the measurements of LDL- and HDL-cholesterol level which correspond to no risk, increased risk and a high risk of developing heart disease.

Table 3.1   Risk and cholesterol (all figures are expressed as mg %)

	No risk	Increased risk	High risk
LDL	<150	150-190	>190
HDL (female)	>65	45-65	<45
HDL (male)	>55	35-55	<35

There is no doubt that blood cholesterol is affected by the fat that you eat in your diet. Cholesterol itself, if eaten in foods, has a small and somewhat predictable effect on plasma cholesterol, but this is well controlled by mechanisms designed to keep cholesterol within normal limits. Thus, the effect of dietary fatty acids derived mainly from animal fat is important because of its additional effect on cholesterol levels.

In general, saturated fatty acids raise cholesterol levels and unsaturated fatty acids either have no effect or lower total cholesterol levels.

How then does the consumption of saturated fats influence the development of atherosclerosis? It has been found that eating large amounts of saturated fatty acids gives rise to cholesterol esters containing these fatty acids, which are then resistant to being broken down. Their presence at the arterial wall will potentiate their accumulation in the arterial wall. More evidence in support of this is produced by substituting the saturated fatty acid with a polyunsaturated fatty acid in the LCAT reaction, which increases the breakdown of cholesterol esters and removal from the site of formation of the fatty deposit.

This lends support to the recommendations that we increase polyunsaturated fatty acids in our diet as a substitute for saturated fatty acids. This is, however, a controversial area in nutrition and much debate has taken place both here and in the United States on the merits of this substitution for the general population. Scientific reports which deal with the role of dietary fat in atherosclerosis are abundant and often contradictory. There is not always a straightforward relationship between the consumption of saturated fats and the development of heart disease. Many experiments have been performed to study the effect of feeding polyunsaturated fatty acids as a preventive measure, but due to poor design most of these studies did not produce conclusive results. There are numerous studies which show no difference in long-term feeding of polyunsaturates compared to saturated fatty acids and often the results with saturated fats were better than those with polyunsaturated fatty acids.

Early 1984 saw the publication of the report by the National Advisory Committee on Nutritional Education (NACNE) in Britain. This committee was set up under the chairmanship of Professor James of the Rowett Institute in Aberdeen and its report was the outcome of discussions between doctors, nutritionists and educational experts. The results of the work of this committee include some recommendations with regard to dietary fat and heart disease. The overall message is that, as a nation, we should eat less fat. The total amount of fat in our diet should provide no more than 30 per cent of the total calories consumed in food and drink, which is a reduction from the present 38 per cent of the total calories. The report follows this by suggesting that saturated fat should not exceed 10 per cent of the total calories, which means reducing a normal intake of saturated fat by a half. With regard to cholesterol intake the committee suggests that if the guidelines for fat are followed then dietary cholesterol should not be a problem.

There is a good deal of consistent evidence that controlling the plasma fats through a control on the amount of fat in the diet can result in a reduction in the risk of atherosclerosis in some people. The aim should be to reduce VLDL- and LDL-cholesterol levels by at least 15 per cent while maintaining or increasing HDL-cholesterol levels. In order to achieve these objectives total cholesterol should be reduced to less than 6.5 mmol/litre, fasting triglycerides to less than 2 mmol/litre and increasing the HDL/LDL cholesterol ratio to more than 2. How this can be achieved by dietary means alone will be discussed in Chapter 5.

Thrombosis

There is an important relationship between atherosclerosis and the development of a blood clot that can lead to a heart attack. The process by which blood clots are formed is called thrombosis and the clot itself is referred to scientifically as a thrombus. As we pointed out earlier, if a blood clot blocks the coronary artery which supplies the heart, it will stop beating and consequently cut off the blood supply to the rest of the body. What we would like to examine now is how a blood clot is thought to form in a vessel that has been subject to fatty deposits through atherosclerosis.

It is thought that the local deposits of cholesterol and other lipids cause a break in the surface of the vessel. The body recognizes any break of this sort in the same way that it recognizes a cut to the outside of the skin. It tries to block the hole with substances that are normally dissolved in the blood. After the initial covering of the hole has taken place, specialized cells in the blood called platelets stick to this area and a blood clot is produced.

How then do the fats influence the production of a blood clot? Some research studies that have been carried out on this problem (and they are few and far between) suggest that saturated fats are more likely to encourage the formation of a clot, and that polyunsaturated fats positively discourage clot formation. This is related to the observation made in the previous chapter that eating polyunsaturated fats increases the time that it takes for the blood to clot. The polyunsaturated fatty acid known as linoleic acid has a specific effect on the formation of a clot. Figure 3.7 shows the effect of different fats on obstruction times.

From Figure 3.7 you can see that by increasing the saturated fatty acid, palmitic acid, the time taken for the blood clot is decreased. In other words the vessel is obstructed quickly by a clot in comparison to a monounsaturated fatty acid (oleic acid), which takes longer to clot. When the amount of linoleic acid, a

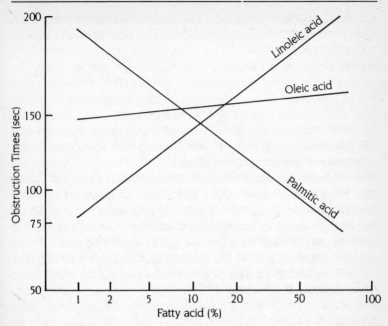

Figure 3.7   Fatty acids and obstruction times. (Reprinted with permission from Elsevier Scientific by A. Hornsha.)

polyunsaturated fatty acid, is increased, then the time taken for the vessel to be obstructed is also increased substantially, thus slowing down the process which forms the clot.

When these clots occur in the vessel wall overlying a plaque the actual sticking of the clot is related to the surface property of the vessel wall. Essential fatty acids, of which linoleic is one, and their metabolites, are important components of the wall and are of vital importance in its function. It may be that increased amounts of saturated fatty acids in the wall makes the platelets over-adhesive, whereas the correct amount of linoleic acid allows the adhesion and aggregation to occur as a normal response to injury.

This normal process might also be affected by impaired prostaglandin production. Prostaglandins are compounds which are important in the control of platelet aggregation. The clotting time is controlled by the balance between two types of prostaglandins. The prevailing hypothesis is that under normal conditions these two types control platelet aggregation and if this balance is upset in favour of the pro-clotting agent then a thrombus can be formed.

Platelet function can be modified through diet because the precursors for the clotting agents' synthesis are the essential fatty acids. This was noted in Eskimos who have a high marine oil, low-fibre diet and also have a low incidence of heart attacks. Their intake of fish is very high and therefore their diet is rich in the fatty acid eicosapentaenoic acid (EPA), which acts as a starting point in the synthesis of the anti-clotting agents.

In addition, the major polyunsaturated fatty acid in the British diet is gamma-linolenic acid, which is the precursor of EPA and will stimulate the production of a pro-clotting agent. So an increased intake in this class of polyunsaturated fatty acids will ensure that the capacity of platelets to produce the pro-clotting agent and of healthy arteries to produce the anti-clotting agent will be at a maximum, and the balance between the two will be finely tuned and neither will dominate.

Obesity

Britain is putting on weight! Approximately one in three adults is overweight and, in general, more men than women are overweight. Whether you put on weight or not is not simply a matter of saying that you eat an excessive amount of food and therefore you will put on weight. Other factors such as heredity, environment, emotional stress and social influences are important. What is true to say is that if you eat more food than is required for your own particular needs, then the excess of food will be stored as fat deposits.

Although research has provided some evidence about a possible cause for an imbalance in obese people between caloric intake and energy output, there is at present no clear reason why they should be singled out as obese individuals. Obesity is a condition in which there is an excessive storage of fat. A reflection of how overweight you are can be assessed from your weight. This obviously depends on your height and here is a weight/height chart to see how you fare.

Men

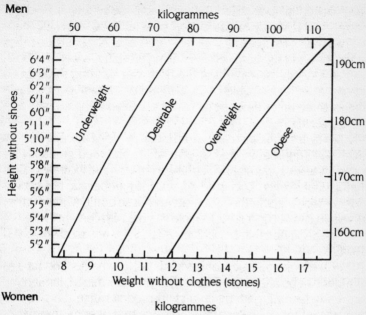

Women

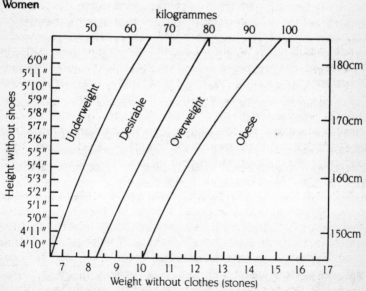

Figure 3.8 Height/weight relationship. (Reprinted with permission from Pan Books by A. Maryon-Davis and J. Thomas.)

Fat is stored in specialized cells (the adipose tissue) around the body — this is what you would think of as fat under the skin. There are two ways of increasing your fat stores: either by filling up these cells; or by adding more cells and filling these up as well. In obese people the total fat content of the body can be up to three times more than in lean people and it is found that obese people have almost three times as many fat cells as do lean people, and these are bigger too.

How do fat cells increase in number in life? Fat cells rapidly increase in number in the first year of life and then gradually up to the thirteenth year, after which time a further rapid increase occurs during adolescence. During adulthood the numbers do not appear to increase except in the moderate-to-obese adult, where further increases can occur. It is impossible to state with certainty whether the increase in the number of fats cells can be reversed or slowed down.

The fundamental question remains as to whether the fat cell number can be altered or if obesity is predetermined. It might be that early feeding patterns in a child predetermine the size and numbers of fat cells. Research indicates that altering the diet of adult obese people does not alter the number of fat cells but merely reduces their size, even if the reduction in weight continues over a long time. This finding suggests that it is important to prevent obesity developing at an early stage in child development. Once the cells have been formed they are a potential store for excess fat in the future.

Obesity *per se* may not be detrimental to overall health but chronic disease is more widespread in obese than in normal people. Obesity carries with it an increased risk of developing conditions which include raised blood fat levels, gallstones, gout, diabetes and high blood pressure. It should be noted that a few of these were listed as risk factors for heart disease.

Diabetes

Diabetes is a disease which is associated with disturbances in the regulation of blood sugar levels. If you eat a meal containing carbohydrate, insulin will be released into the bloodstream and this helps the sugars to be absorbed into the cells of the body. At the same time the insulin prevents the fats from being broken down. If you consider this as a system, it is logical. The body uses the sugar that is readily available in the meal straight away for its energy needs and keeps the fats in reserve for a 'rainy day'.

Where this system goes wrong is in the adult form of diabetes. In this disease the cells seem unable to take up the sugar, but they are still prevented from breaking down the fat. Adult-onset diabetes is associated with the decreased sensitivity of receptors which allow glucose and other sugars to be taken up into the cells. Thus, more insulin, the hormone that aids glucose uptake, is produced. This hormone also inhibits fat breakdown and as a consequence more fat is stored than is normal. The fat cells in this disease are similar in appearance to those described in the obese person, and certainly this type of diabetes is associated with obesity. One way of avoiding the overloading with fat in this type of diabetes is by a strict regulation of dietary fat.

This is an over-simplification of the various metabolic processes that are involved in adult-onset diabetes. It can be appreciated, however, that the general effects of this disease lead to increased levels of circulating fat and may well lead to the development of heart disease through the mechanisms already outlined earlier in this chapter.

Gallstone Disease

The cholesterol levels in tissues throughout the body are finely controlled between its synthesis, dietary cholesterol, tissue levels and excretion of cholesterol and its metabolites. Its metabolism has already been discussed in Chapter 1 and here a disease involved with cholesterol excretion is described.

As we stated earlier, lipids — of which cholesterol is an example — are normally insoluble in water. Cholesterol is kept soluble in the bile by being associated with phospholipids and bile acids. A feature of all substances is that they have a certain limited solubility, i.e. even substances such as sugar will only dissolve to a certain extent in water. If you add a large amount of sugar to water not all of it will dissolve. In the same way, if a large excess of cholesterol is present in the bile it will not be able to dissolve but it will come out of solution in the form of a solid. When this happens in the gallbladder, or other parts of the biliary system, deposits are formed which are referred to as gallstones.

Gallstone disease is characterized by the presence of these cholesterol deposits called stones in the biliary system. Most gallstones have a very high percentage of cholesterol which forms crystals. The formation of these stones occurs if the relative amounts of bile acids, cholesterol and phospholipids are not favourable for cholesterol solubility, i.e. if the bile contains an excess of cholesterol or contains reduced amounts of bile acids and/or phospholipids.

Supersaturation of bile with cholesterol results from a metabolic defect in the liver and may be due to excessive synthesis and excretion of cholesterol, which predominates in the obese. More commonly, gallstones can form as a result of reduced bile acid synthesis, leading to a lower bile acid concentration in the bile, together with a reduction in phospholipids. Risk factors known to increase the incidence of gallstones are obesity, with the associated increased blood cholesterol, late adult life, femaleness and diabetes.

As saturated phospholipid can hold less cholesterol it has been thought that eating polyunsaturated fats or phospholipids might enhance the solubility of cholesterol and prevent gallstone formation. Polyunsaturated phospholipid fed to rats can increase the bile flow and cholesterol excretion, with an accompanying increase in linoleic acid in bile. The opposite occurred with egg lecithin, which contains predominantly saturated fatty acids.

The phospholipid part of bile is mainly phosphatidylcholine and can either contain saturated or unsaturated fatty acids. Due to their shape differences, and ability to hold cholesterol, patients with gallstones were fed lecithin. There is some evidence to suggest that unsaturated lecithin does increase bile flow and cholesterol excretion in these patients, possibly due to an increase in the unsaturated fatty acid content of bile.

General Harmful Effects of Fats

There have been studies in recent years at an international level that have produced some evidence for dietary factors having an involvement in the development of certain human cancers. It was noted that in the United States in the last thirty years the incidence of breast and colon cancers has increased at a time when polyunsaturated fat intake has also increased, although a strong correlation has not been shown, mainly owing to lack of studies.

Animal studies on the effect of diet on tumour development have shown that high levels of dietary fat will promote cancer cell growth. Diets high in polyunsaturated fats were more effective in promoting growth than diets high in saturated fats. It has been suggested that polyunsaturated fats might have an effect on the way carcinogens (cancer-promoting agents) are metabolized by affecting the enzymes involved in this process. Confirmation of these animal studies in humans, to relate fat intake to cancer, has not been published but there is a need for more investigations into the role, if any, of fats in cancer.

Another aspect of the harmful effects of fats in the diet is that many commercial margarine products contain trans-fatty acids. These are formed during the manufacturing process of some margarines from vegetable oils, and can contribute up to 20-50 per cent of the fatty acids in some vegetable oils. Saturated fats contain only 1-5 per cent of trans-fatty acids, mainly as a result of the animal eating vegetable products. The difference between polyunsaturated fatty acids in the cis- and trans- forms are in relation to the rate at which they are metabolized. The trans-fatty acids are not metabolized normally compared to the cis-fatty acids. They are preferentially stored and can account for up to 14 per cent of the fat in human tissues. Clearly, if these unusual fatty acids accumulate in the tissues of the body they will have effects on the metabolism of quite a few substances. Some of our enzymes are bound to cell membranes and, by altering the fatty acid composition of the membrane, it can be expected that enzyme activity will be affected. Again, further studies need to be undertaken to clarify the effects of trans-fatty acid on our bodies and in relation to any disease state.

There are a few fatty acids which, if taken in large quantities, have potentially toxic effects. The levels of the fatty acids taken in our normal diet do not have any toxic effects, but they are mentioned here because they are all contained in edible oils. Cottonseed oil contains a fatty acid called cyclopropene acid which comprises about 0.1-0.5 per cent of the oil for our consumption. Cyclopropene acid is toxic to humans, but the content in present day cottonseed oil is too low to have an effect.

Rapeseed oil contains a fatty acid called erucic acid, which constitutes more than 40 per cent of the total fatty acids in this oil. An increased use of rapeseed oil in some countries in salad oils, cooking oils, margarine and shortening has made the public aware of the toxic effects of erucic acid on heart muscle. Due to this these countries have limited the content of erucic aicd in rapeseed oil. Some marine oils contain fatty acids similar to erucic acid in their composition and effect. These are also limited in the food we eat.

The food industry keeps a close eye for us on the content of these potentially harmful fatty acids so there is no risk to the general public. They are included here to make you aware that fat is a complex ingredient in our diet and that it is not always the total amount of fat which will affect us, but also the characteristics of the individual fats and their fatty acids.

Summary

Disturbances in fat metabolism are associated with the development of a number of 'Western' diseases which have been described in this chapter, i.e. atherosclerosis, thrombosis, obesity, diabetes, gallstone disease and general harmful effects. A complicated picture emerges where individual diseases have some features characteristic of another and increase the risk of that second disease, for example, obesity and diabetes. Evidence for the effect of dietary fat as the cause of these diseases is not conclusive, but fat metabolism is affected in all of them whether by diet or otherwise. Current nutrition research now asks the question 'What is the optimum fat composition in the diet?'

4

Other Factors Affecting Fat Metabolism

So far we have examined what fats are, in some detail, followed by a review of the various disease states that can arise from disturbances in fat metabolism. You need to appreciate the background to fats before you can start making positive changes to your diet. This chapter sets out to build upon this knowledge base and to use it to examine the way in which we can alter the fat in our body through diet, including dietary supplements and by a variety of other means.

By summarizing the medical evidence it becomes clear that the claims of advertisers are not always supported by concrete research. There is one example that is often quoted in newspapers, that of switching from butter to margarine. You might be forgiven for thinking that switching from butter to margarine could help you to lose weight. But we have shown earlier, butter contains the same number of calories as margarine. Simply substituting margarine for butter does not help you to lose weight if you eat the equivalent amount of margarine. Where the switch is important is in the substitution of saturated fats (in butter) for the polyunsaturated fats (in certain branded margarines).

There has recently been a considerable amount of press coverage on the subject of fat, cholesterol and heart disease. In particular, 1984 saw the publication of the 'NACNE' report explained in detail in *The Food Scandal* (G. Cannon and C. Walker), *Diet 2000* (A. Maryon-Davis and J. Thomas) and the completion of an investigation in the United States into the cholesterol-lowering drug called cholestyramine.

The NACNE report recommended that total fat, and particularly saturated fat, should be reduced significantly. As stated earlier this means reducing total fat intake from the present 40 per cent of total calories to 30-35 per cent of the total. Here we will discuss measures which are available that have beneficial effects on fat metabolism and that you can try yourself.

Diet

Most of us are vaguely aware of what we eat and drink even if it is too much of both. Fat and happy — how often have we heard someone say that?

There have been many books published in the last few years on *the* best way to lose weight, most of them proposing a miracle cure for slimmers. Witness the 'Scarsdale Diet', the 'Beverley Hills Diet' and the 'F-Plan Diet'. This section examines the basis of these diets in relation to fat consumption.

Firstly, you need to appreciate how a good diet is worked out. The best way of designing a diet is to examine what effect it has on normal human subjects. This is called a 'dietary trial'. The subject is given a foodstuff which is either the one under investigation or a dummy which looks and tastes the same but is known by previous trials to exert no effect. This is called a double-blind study, such

that the investigator and the subject are unaware of which is which. Another researcher is aware of the nature of the foodstuff being given but does not allow the primary investigator to know the details until the trial has been completed. This ensures that the person carrying out the measurements does not exert a subjective assessment of the potential effects during the trial. In order to examine the effects of the diet on fat metabolism, blood samples may be taken at regular intervals and measurements made in the laboratory of changes in fat parameters. We have conducted a number of these trials and the results will be used in order to explain the effects that diet has on fat metabolism.

Attention will initially be directed towards the fat in our diet and how it affects the fat in our bodies. As you are now aware the fatty acids in dietary lipids can be split into three classes: saturated, monounsaturated and polyunsaturated. These three have different effects on fat metabolism, which will now be described.

Saturated Fats

The brief analysis of fatty acid composition of foodstuffs given in Chapter 1 should alert you to the fact that foods contain a mixture of different types of fatty acids. It would be convenient to say that all you need to do is to modify one particular fat component and then you have the ideal diet. But as foods are a complex mixture of fats, you have to bear in mind the *overall* effect of the fat, and this means having to consider both the type and amount of fat that is eaten. Table 4.1 shows the composition of some typical fats which contain a high proportion of saturated fatty acids. The examples chosen are intended to indicate certain types of foods. For beef fat, for example, you could substitute pork fat or lamb fat in the table and have a similar fatty acid composition.

Table 4.1   Fatty acid content in some fats
% total fatty acid

Fatty acid	12:0	14:0	16:0	18:0	20:0	MUFA	PUFA
Fat							
Coconut oil	48	16	9	12	1	7	2
Cocoa butter	0	0	25	33	1	32	3
Butter fat	2	10	26	12	1	29	4
Beef fat	Trace	3	21	13	Trace	48	4

12:0 — lauric acid   20:0 — a long chain saturated fatty
14:0 — myristic acid   acid
16:0 — palmitic acid   MUFA — monounsaturated fatty acid
18:0 — stearic acid   PUFA — polyunsaturated fatty acid

The difficulty in determining the effect of a particular fatty acid is compounded by the fact that most dietary trials are conducted with purified fatty acid preparations. In general, however, we are able to see trends in the effects that fatty acids have on blood cholesterol levels. Stearic acid (18:0) raises blood cholesterol levels less than palmitic acid (16:0). The shorter chain fatty acids, for example, myristic (14:0) raise serum cholesterol levels more than palmitic or stearic acids. The general conclusion is that short chain fatty acids raise blood cholesterol more than long chain fatty acids.

In considering the overall effect of the fatty acid it is important to consider the other accompanying fatty acids in the food. It is not good enough to say that if a food contains a significant amount of saturated fats it is going to increase the blood levels of cholesterol. What you can say with some degree of certainty is that if you eat a diet that contains a predominantly high proportion of saturated fatty acids, without an equivalent amount of unsaturated fats, then *overall* it will increase the level of blood cholesterol.

There is considerable evidence in the medical literature that fats containing predominantly saturated fatty acids increase cholesterol levels in the blood and that the individual acids vary substantially in their effect. The issue is not entirely clearcut, as the effect, for example, of stearic acid depends on the conditions and source of the acid. This is important as the principle source of stearic acid in our modern diet is from meat. Fats such as butter fat and coconut oil will be very effective at raising cholesterol levels. Whether this is due to their specific fatty acid effect content, or total amount of fat, is of less practical importance than designing diets around agents which do not raise cholesterol levels.

Polyunsaturated Fats

Throughout this book we have hinted at the beneficial effects of polyunsaturated fatty acids on fat metabolism. There is an abundance of research evidence which supports the view that polyunsaturated fats have a 'cholesterol-lowering effect', although the precise mechanism by which they exert their effect remains obscure. There are a number of ways that the effect can be produced; these are — by decreasing the absorption of cholesterol, by affecting the distribution and metabolism of cholesterol, and by increasing the excretion of cholesterol. It is probably a combination of these processes that governs the 'cholesterol-lowering effect'.

Our own research indicates that polyunsaturated fats can reduce the amount of cholesterol that is absorbed from the diet. The precise process needs to be clarified but it appears that the polyunsaturated fatty acid exerts a physical effect at this level and acts as a barrier to absorption.

Quite a lot of research has been conducted on the distribution of cholesterol. You will recall from Chapter 2 that we showed how cholesterol is carried in significant amounts in both LDL and HDL. If the cholesterol is carried in LDL, it is able to enter cells of the body by a specific recognition system (receptor-mediated uptake). If the cholesterol is carried in HDL then it is not able to be taken up by cells by this mechanism and is consequently dispersed in another way. This is thought to speed up the excretion of cholesterol. But do polyunsaturated fatty acids help to load up the HDL particles and consequently increase the clearance of cholesterol from the bloodstream?

It seems that HDL is ingeniously designed to cope with this problem. This lipoprotein starts its life in the bloodstream as a cigar-shaped object. As it progresses through the bloodstream it takes cholesterol from the surrounding medium on to its surface. The enzyme LCAT (see page 42) then converts the cholesterol to cholesterol ester. In this form, as the cholesterol ester, it is able to sit in the middle of the `cigar', whereas the cholesterol had to sit on the edge of the `cigar'. As more and more cholesterol is converted to the cholesterol ester the cigar shape becomes more of a ball shape. If the cholesterol ester has been generated from a polyunsaturated fatty acid then the ball can accommodate a much larger amount of material. In general we can think of the HDL particle as a `scavenger' for cholesterol — it mops up any that is available to it and consequently aids its removal from the bloodstream to other areas where the effects of cholesterol are less pronounced.

When we look at the results of clinical trials, where polyunsaturated fats have been taken in large amounts, the results are often not as striking as one might expect. The reductions obtained in blood cholesterol concentrations are often quite good in patients who have high blood cholesterol levels to start off with. In `normal' patients the effects are far less dramatic. This is mentioned in order to exert a cautionary note in deciding that polyunsaturated fats are beneficial in every case. There is undoubtedly a benefit that can be obtained in substituting polyunsaturated fats for saturated fats in small amounts, but it would be unwise to suggest that you should replace all of the saturated fats in your diet.

What foods provide the richest souce of polyunsaturated fats? You can see from Table 4.2 that vegetable oils contain a high proportion of linoleic acid, the exception being olive oil which contains predominantly oleic acid.

Table 4.1   Fatty acid content of vegetable oils

% total fatty acid

Fatty acid	SFA	16:1	18:1	20:1	22:1	18:2	18:3
Oil							
Olive	15	1	72	0	0	11	1
Soyabean	15	0	25	0	Trace	52	7
Safflower	11	0	13	0	0	75	1

16:1 — palmitoleic acid   22:1 — a long chain mono-
18:1 — oleic acid   unsaturated fatty acid
20:1 — a long chain mono-   18:2 — linoleic acid
           unsaturated fatty acid   18:3 — linolenic acid
                                                   SFA — saturated fatty acids

It is worthwhile at this point to consider another mechanism whereby the polyunsaturated fatty acid known as linoleic acid exerts a beneficial effect, i.e. on the functioning of platelets. We mentioned earlier that platelets are cells in the bloodstream that are important in the clotting of blood. There is a fine balance between the ability of blood to clot in response to injury and maintaining a normal blood flow through healthy blood vessels. If blood clots easily this is good from the point of view of preventing excessive blood loss when the skin is broken but it also means that there is an increased risk of developing blood clots in healthy blood vessels which, eventually, may lead to a heart attack.

Linoleic acid is converted by the body into a molecule that is known to inhibit the clumping together of platelets and hence prevents the clotting of the blood. What happens initially is that linoleic acid is converted to dihomo-gamma-linolenic acid and arachidonic acid, both of which are precursors for the active molecules. This might explain why arachidonic acid and gamma-linolenic acid are often quoted as being beneficial in preventing heart disease in the same way as linoleic acid.

Further evidence that dietary fats modify platelet function and the clotting mechanism has been published on fish oil, which is rich in a polyunsaturated fatty acid called eicosapentaenoic acid that also opposes the clotting process. It promotes the manufacture of the active component in the process which inhibits clotting.

These observations on various fatty acids have a bearing on the often reported recommendation of replacing butter with margarine to prevent heart disease. Most margarines contain linoleic acid in varying amounts, depending on the brand. This can be converted to an inhibitor of blood clotting, as discussed earlier, but the trans-linoleic acid also present in margarines has a different effect and is not converted to this compound. These trans-fatty acids are easily transformed to a peroxidized form and these act like saturated fats and allow platelet clotting to be stimulated.

Thus, certain constituents of margarines can be potentially harmful in terms of platelet clotting and hence heart disease. It must be emphasized that a change to specific fatty acids, such as linoleic acid, is far more beneficial than a generalized switch to consumption of unsaturated fats.

Dietary Cholesterol

This has for many years been presented to the public as the `*agent provacateur*' in heart disease. Most people have heard about cholesterol and have gained the impression that if they eat foods which are low in cholesterol or cholesterol-free then this will automatically lower the blood cholesterol. Conversely, (largely as a result of the margarine campaign) if foods are eaten that are rich in cholesterol then this will result in high levels of blood cholesterol. But is this really true?

If we look at what happens in animals who are fed modified diets the results can be quite dramatic. Rabbits fed diets containing 2-3 per cent of cholesterol (per weight of food) develop very high levels of blood cholesterol, particularly in the LDL fraction. Their major blood vessels quickly show signs of fatty deposits and this led some researchers to the conclusion that this was a good model of the human situation with regard to atherosclerosis. The disease produced by cholesterol feeding in rabbits is, however, a storage disease and cannot be scientifically related to the human disease, which is more than just a storage disease.

Most researchers now consider that dietary cholesterol alone has a small effect on blood cholesterol levels in normal people. There are many control systems in the process of absorption, metabolism and excretion of cholesterol that are used to balance out the amount of cholesterol in the blood. Strangely enough then, dietary cholesterol seems to have only a small effect on blood cholesterol and other factors, such as the consumption of saturated fats, appear to be more important.

This can be seen in the matter of eating eggs, which contain a high cholesterol concentration. Vegetarians given one egg per day, in addition to the normal diet, increased the cholesterol concentration of the blood to begin with but after eight weeks the blood cholesterol levels had returned to their starting values. It is now generally agreed that a healthy, active individual can eat eggs as a normal part of a balanced diet without suffering a massive increase in blood cholesterol levels. There may be an initial increase in blood cholesterol but the body compensates by reducing the amount it makes.

There is also a fallacy that eating eggs is alright because eggs contain lecithin, i.e. phosphatidylcholine, but the fatty acid chains in this case are of the saturated type and, as we have already shown, saturated fats do not reduce cholesterol levels. What is important is that the body compensates for the increased cholesterol intake by reducing the amount of cholesterol that it makes.

Protein

Relatively little attention has been focused on the role of dietary protein on lipid metabolism, as most of the research effect has concentrated on dietary fat. This is somewhat surprising when it is fairly well accepted that vegetarians have lower blood fat levels than people who eat meat. This could, however, be related to the vegetarian's reduced saturated fat intake as well as the lack of meat.

Blood cholesterol can be reduced by substituting plant protein for animal protein in the diet, although this effect is not always found. People with raised cholesterol levels respond more to plant protein in the diet than people with normal cholesterol levels, and this has given rise to some confusion.

The mechanism by which dietary protein can affect blood cholesterol is not understood. It has been shown that the conversion of cholesterol to its excretory products, the bile acids, is slower in animals fed animal protein rather than plant protein, which leads to an increased blood cholesterol. This gives rise to the possibility that protein exerts an effect on blood cholesterol through somehow slowing the rate of cholesterol metabolism and excretion.

Fibre

In the last ten years interest has grown in the role of dietary fibre on fat metabolism. Fibre (or roughage) in the diet is that material taken in our food which is not digested in our intestine and therefore passes through the body unaltered. This category includes the majority of plant cells, with a few exceptions, and consists mostly of complex sugars.

The interest in fibre has developed because of the observation that populations with different eating habits to those of the West, particularly with regard to fibre consumption, have vastly different incidences of fat-related diseases. The higher the fibre content in the diet the lower the incidence of the so-called 'Western' diseases described in Chapter 3. In this country, the recent NACNE report recommends that we increase our fibre intake to more than 30 grams per day. Fibre content is high in foods such as fresh fruit, particularly if you eat their skins. Breakfast cereal and baked potatoes with vegetables would supply most people's needs as far as fibre is concerned.

The main effect that fibre has in the intestine, which will affect fat metabolism, is waterholding and absorption of certain compounds in the gut. The effect of its waterholding ability on fat results in an alteration of absorption and digestion of fat. An increase in some types of fibre in the diet results in an increase in excretion in fat from the diet, and body fats such as cholesterol and bile acids, its excretory products. This ability to absorb bile acids is thought to be the main way in which fibre affects fat metabolism. Fat is then lost in the bile acids due to a decrease in reabsorption, which should take place in the intestine. As the bile acids are then not available for fat and cholesterol absorption, then this will also be lost to the body.

Giving increased amounts of dietary fibre to people has had a variety of effects on fat metabolism and depends mainly on the type and source of the fibre. Wheat bran and cellulose consistently have no effect on blood cholesterol or triglyceride. In contrast pectin, found in apples and used as the setting agent in jams and jellies, decreases blood cholesterol levels, as a result of increased excretion of cholesterol and bile acids. Although wheat bran had no effect on blood cholesterol it did have an effect in the intestine in that it binds bile acids.

Our understanding of the involvement of dietary fibre in fat metabolism is still quite limited, although there is a strong suggestion that it combines with bile acids and as a consequence alters cholesterol and bile acid balance. This effect is involved when a blood cholesterol reduction is seen with some of these types of fibre. However, not all types of fibre that we eat in our diet have these effects so we need to be a bit cautious in assuming that all fibre will lower cholesterol levels.

Alcohol

A little of what you fancy does you good — but does it? It is well known that over-consumption of alcohol certainly does you harm by causing liver and heart damage. However, as a result of a long survey in the United States, some beneficial effects of alcohol have been observed. Of particular relevance to us is the conclusion that alcohol has some effect on fat metabolism.

The study was conducted over a twenty year period such that the drinking habits of men over this time could be tied in with heart disease. The results are presented in Figure 4.2 which shows the incidence of heart disease in relation to alcohol consumption in ounces per month. So that you can relate the alcohol consumption to drinks per month there is also a table showing the content of well-known drinks.

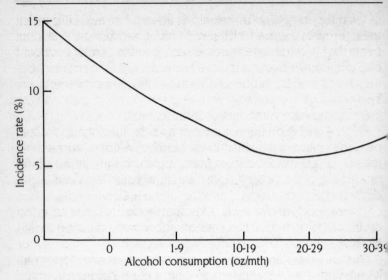

Figure 4.2 The effect of alcohol on heart disease

Table 4.3 Alcohol content

Drink	Amount	Alcohol (g)	Alcohol (oz)
Beer	1 pint	17.4	0.60
Lager	1 pint	18.2	0.64
Wine	1 glass	19.0	0.67
Gin	⅛ gill	15.8	0.56

From Figure 4.2 you can see that moderate drinking is associated with a decreased risk of heart disease. But beware, because careful inspection of the graph will reveal that when alcohol consumption is above 29 ounces per month then the risk of heart disease also increases.

This study stimulated a lot of research into the mechanism whereby alcohol could have any such protective action on heart disease. It was noted that alcohol intake is associated with an increased HDL-cholesterol, which is considered to be beneficial in heart disease for reasons discussed earlier.

In another study normal healthy subjects were given half a bottle of wine per day (40-45 grams alcohol) for six weeks, after which the intake was reduced. HDL-cholesterol rose during the alcohol period but fell again afterwards. It was also noted that the amount of cholesterol in bile was reduced with alcohol consumption, but this also returned to its previous level after the alcohol was reduced. This could be associated with a decreased risk of gallstones to people who have a moderate drinking habit.

Alcohol has also been shown to have an anti-clotting effect in people given very high quantities of alcohol. Alcohol stopped the release of phospholipid from platelets, which then inhibited the production of the clotting agents but it had no effect on the anti-clotting agents.

However, before everyone goes out and thinks they can safely drink alcohol with not a care in the world, a word of caution! High intakes of alcohol of more than a half a bottle of wine a day (or more than 2½ pints beer) causes an increase in triglyceride, impairs fat absorption in the intestine, and promotes fat synthesis in the fat tissue and liver — resulting in a fatty liver. This is thought to occur because alcohol has an effect on some of the enzymes involved in fat metabolism.

Alcohol is a double-edged weapon. A moderate intake will have beneficial results in terms of heart disease and gallstones, but the multiplicity of the effects of alcohol makes it difficult to recommend it for therapeutic use. So the message on alcohol is still that you can drink a little but too much is harmful!

Exercise

Exercise is good for you! The Health Education Council has made a concerted effect in broadcasting the benefits of daily exercise. It has shown that:

1. Exercise improves the staying power of your heart and circulation;
2. It keeps joints supple and improves posture;
3. It tightens muscles and improves strength;
4. It helps to keep you slim;
5. It helps to combat stress;
6. It can be fun!

In relation to the effects of exercise on fat metabolism, in particular, recent investigations have begun to unravel the mechanisms that are involved. The benefit obtained through exercise seems to be directly related to the amount of exercise undertaken, i.e. whether it is active or not and how often it is taken. It should be clear from our previous discussion that anything that reduces total cholesterol and increases HDL-cholesterol is potentially beneficial in lowering the risk of developing heart disease in both men and women.

In general, athletes are found to have lower total cholesterol and raised HDL-cholesterol levels. Strenuous exercise can result in as much as a 20-35 per cent increase in HDL-cholesterol. The effects on LDL-cholesterol are smaller. The overall effects of exercise on blood cholesterol are summarized in Figure 4.3, the results being expressed as percentage change.

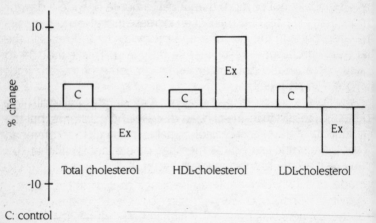

C: control
Ex: exercise

Figure 4.3   The effect of exercise on cholesterol levels. (Reprinted with permission from Grune & Stratton Inc. by P. D. Wood *et al.*)

How does exercise bring about these changes? It seems almost too obvious to point out that exercise requires a large expenditure of energy. This probably increases the rate at which the lipoproteins are metabolized. The enzyme LCAT is known to be more active during training, which results in an increased cholesterol concentration in the HDL fraction. Because of its role in scavenging for cholesterol, an increase in this fraction will lead to an increased removal of cholesterol from the bloodstream.

However, these changes cannot be considered as permanent. If the exercise is stopped then there is evidence that the body reverts to its normal pre-exercise state. This was shown clearly in a study on oarsmen who had a seven-month training period followed by a rest period of five months. During the training phase or 'active' phase their HDL-cholesterol levels increased, total cholesterol decreased and triglyceride levels also dropped. During the 'off' season the fats reverted to their pre-training values, which were no different from their non-trained colleagues. The message should be that, to be of maximum effect, exercise has to be taken regularly.

It is not all types of exercise that produce beneficial effects in relation to lipid metabolism. Athletes who train for strength and power events also consume large quantities of food to compensate for the energy lost in exercise. In this case it is often found that total cholesterol actually increases. This is a rare situation, as most people who exercise do not go in for this sort of training, but it is worth pointing out as you have to pick the type of exercise to suit your needs.

Another cautionary note needs to be sounded at this stage, namely, that when considering an exercise programme it is best to start slowly and surely. This is particularly important if you are overweight or potentially at risk of developing heart disease. It is wise then to consult your doctor so that an assessment can be made as to whether you are fit enough to start some vigorous activity. The risks of overdoing exercise to a person already aware of the dangers was poignantly highlighted in July 1984 with the sudden death of James Fixx, who promoted jogging in the United States. He ran ten miles every day, even though he was suffering from chest pains. It is thought that he persisted with this programme despite the chest pains and breathlessness and died of heart failure whilst out running.

Fitness does not always equate with health but we should beware of swinging to the opposite viewpoint that exercise is dangerous to health. For the normal population, exercise in a controlled way is both beneficial and fun. As well as having recognized good effects in metabolism it improves the quality of life.

Dietary Supplements

There are some special products sold in the shops, particularly health food shops, which are advertised as being 'health-giving'. One of the means by which they are supposed to be beneficial to our health is through their effect on fat metabolism. Two such products will now be described — lecithin and evening primrose oil.

Lecithin

The term lecithin refers specifically to phosphatidylcholine, although it is often used to refer to that mixture of phospholipids that can be extracted from soya beans and other sources rich in phospholipids. Soyabean lecithin is the product most commonly found in health food shops, and for the purposes of this book phosphatidylcholine and soya lecithin are the same thing. Lecithin contains a high proportion of the fatty acid linoleic acid, although there are a number of other fatty acids in the product.

It is worth pointing out that lecithin is found in a great many foodstuffs and the fatty acid composition depends on the source of the material. It is widely used in the food industry because of its ability to act as an emulsification agent, i.e. it binds foodstuffs together and facilitates the mixing of otherwise insoluble components with water. To this end it may be mixed with vegetable oils to generate margarines and low-fat spreads. It is extensively used in the preparation of chocolate, cooking fats and ice cream. What is discussed below relates specifically to soya lecithin, which is widely used in the food industry, but it also relates to the fact that soya lecithin is very rich in linoleic acid.

Soya lecithin is absorbed from the gut and is distributed by the bloodstream lipoproteins to the tissues and organs of the body. Phosphatidylcholine is one of the molecules that takes part in the LCAT reaction, in which a fatty acid from lecithin is attached to cholesterol. It is, therefore, important in the process by which HDL is loaded up with cholesterol and removed from the circulation. When the fatty acid being transferred to cholesterol is linoleic acid (as will be the case when soya lecithin is in HDL) this will produce a cholesterol ester that is capable of sitting comfortably in the HDL particle. Under these circumstances more cholesterol will be removed from the tissues as HDL can carry more, until the lecithin in HDL is exhausted.

We have already mentioned that dietary lecithin is derived from both natural sources and as an additive to certain foods. Depending on the choice of food the intake of lecithin from natural sources may be 2-3 grams per day. The foodstuffs with the highest content of lecithin are soyabeans, wheat grain, peanuts, beef and some vegetable oils. Most of the consumption from the manufactured products is in margarines, chocolate, cooking fats and ice cream. Using a supplement of lecithin the daily intake can be increased to 10-25 grams per day without any ill effects.

When considering any beneficial effects of lecithin it is important to point out that the source of lecithin will have an influence on this effect. Egg lecithin contains predominantly saturated fatty acids and consequently will supply these to the body, which will in turn have similar effects on blood lipids to those of eating saturated fats. Soya lecithin contains predominantly unsaturated fatty acids and hence its effect on blood lipids will be that of dietary unsaturated fats. It is advertised as a useful food supplement in that it can potentially be helpful in some of the fat-related disorders.

Evening primrose oil

Evening primrose oil is extracted from the plant of the same name. It was in the 1960s that scientists explored the use of this oil for its possible beneficial therapeutic uses and discovered that evening primrose oil was a rich source of a fatty acid called gamma-linolenic acid. At present the yield of gamma-linolenic acid from the plant is 7-9 per cent. The oil is also very rich in linoleic acid (70 per cent) which returns us to the same effect that lecithin has in blood lipids and platelet function (see Chapter 3).

Linoleic acid is converted to molecules that have an effect on blood clotting. Gamma-linolenic acid, the main ingredient of evening primrose oil, is the first molecule made from linoleic acid in this process. The rationale behind giving gamma-linolenic acid, instead of linoleic acid, is that this first step is easily blocked or slowed down by saturated fats, cholesterol and trans-fatty acids in the blood. Bypassing this step will ensure the manufacture of agents involved in the control of blood clotting.

Due to its high linoleic acid content evening primrose oil acts as a source of polyunsaturated fats which has already been shown to maintain low cholesterol levels or even reduce high levels. This will not be rediscussed here except to summarize that the linoleic acid will help to lower LDL-cholesterol but has little effect on HDL-cholesterol.

Thus, evening primrose oil is likely to have an effect on fat metabolism both through its linoleic acid content and its gamma-linolenic acid content, enabling the body to sidestep the conversion of linoleic acid to gamma-linolenic acid.

Summary

Many factors can influence fat metabolism in your body and some of the more commonly known have been described. Your fat stores and metabolism can be changed by the acitvities you enjoy, habits that you keep and your diet. More specifically you can modify your fat by:

1. Dietary manipulation of:
    a) Saturated fat
    b) Polyunsaturated fat
    c) Cholesterol
    d) Protein
    e) Fibre
2. Alcohol
3. Exercise
4. Supplements:
    a) Lecithin
    b) Evening primrose oil

The most important factor to appreciate is that any changes to your daily life can modify your fats and often to good effect *but* overdoing anything can have deleterious consequences, as in the case of alcohol.

5

Planning Your Diet

You should be in no doubt now that fat plays a vital role in health and disease. Returning to Chapter 1, it was mentioned there how difficult it is for anyone to appreciate the fat composition of food just by looking at its outward appearance. The most appropriate phrase that comes to mind is that you 'can't judge a book by its cover'. Now that you know a bit more about food you can begin to look beneath the outward appearance and get to grips with the character of the food in question. The information provided in this chapter should enable you to be far more selective in choosing which items should be included in your diet and which things you could very well do without.

What Is a Diet?

Some people automatically associate 'diet' with slimming or some specialized pattern of eating. Diet here describes the total food that is consumed and, in general, if you eat a wide range of foods in sensible amounts the chances are that you already have an adequate diet. Having a *healthy* balanced diet does not mean that you have to go on a health food kick and eat lots of raw carrots, wholemeal bread and fish — although you can if you want to — it simply means that you take in all the energy and nutrients that the body needs, in the right amount and proportion. This applies to general health, slimming diets and therapeutic diets under a dietician's supervision. Guidelines will be dealt with in a short section later on (see page 92) but in general a week-by-week check on your diet should suffice.

A well-balanced diet ensures that the body receives adequate supplies of protein, carbohydrate, fat, minerals and vitamins for daily life. We have concentrated on fat and, although it must again be stressed that you have to consider this with the rest of your diet, we are going to pick out the fat part of many foods and show you how to quantify it in the foods you eat, and how you can alter the fat content of foods by preparation and cooking methods. We will also give some examples of meals, highlighting the fat content of the total meal, which obviously will include some non-fatty foods in order to show you how you can control your fat intake over the course of a week.

The history of diet-making

It is interesting to review the factors that governed the way in which our Western diet evolved. If we remind ourselves of the cavemen of Chapter 1, we can appreciate that the hunter was mostly concerned with obtaining sufficient food to meet his immediate needs. The preparation and serving of food became a ritual in celebration of the killing. In the evolution of man, and particularly with the onset of industrialization and urbanization, certain features have been carried over that may not be entirely relevant to our modern way of living. Even if we just confine ourselves to the past fifty years, we can see how our attitudes towards diet have changed. We eat a vast range of processed foods and add more in the way of supplementary fats such as butter, margarine and vegetable oils than ever before.

In most Western countries fat provides 35-45 per cent of the total energy in the diet. Fat is mostly added during the preparation and cooking of a meal, but it is also a necessity for a good tasty dish. Most cooks will prepare a meal with materials in which fat supplies at least 20 per cent of the energy. The majority of people would not enjoy their traditional meals if fat was excluded. This was illustrated during World War II when fat in the diet fell to 33 per cent of the diet from a pre-war level of about 39 per cent. After the war it rose steadily to 39 per cent and then to 42 per cent. Many illnesses and the discontent during the war years was attributed to the lack of fat in the diet, although 33 per cent is sufficient for good health. It is clear that the food cooked with less fat was insipid and unpalatable to traditional British tastes. Thus, it can be seen that the fat requirement for 'good living' is higher than that for general health.

The minimum requirement for fat is difficult to assess, as foods which are very low in fat are also low in protein and fat-soluble vitamins. This means that a deficiency disease resulting from a diet low in fat need not necessarily be a fat-deficiency disease *per se*. On the opposite end of the scale, high-fat diets — except in the very active — lead to obesity. A high fat intake can also contribute towards a high incidence of the 'Western' diseases, described in Chapter 3, and should be avoided.

Balancing the Fat Equation

One question often asked is 'how much fat can be regarded as a normal intake?' Unfortunately, this is a question that cannot be answered easily. If we were all the same, it would be just a matter of balancing the fat equation, just like you try to balance your bank account. If you have more in your current account than you require for your daily use, you might deposit surplus cash elsewhere. In a similar way, if you have more energy in your diet than you need for your daily needs, your body will store up the excess as fat for a 'rainy day'. The major problem is that, just as people are variable spenders of cash, we are also variable spenders of energy. During your life there are times when you might use up the reserves fairly easily and other times when you store the excess.

A common way of assessing how much energy you need is to 'count the calories'. Using this method you assume that you require something like 2,500 calories per day and then you add up how much is present in your food (from food tables). If you get the balance right then you will not put on weight. Where most people come unstuck is being able to assess how many calories they need from day to day. The amount will vary daily depending on whether you are active or not. It will also vary individually with the efficiency with which you utilize your food.

Counting calories is fine but you also need to take into consideration the type of food that you eat. In previous chapters we have pointed out that saturated fats have quite a different effect to unsaturated fats in terms of risk of certain diseases. Now we are going to illustrate the content and composition of the fat in various foodstuffs but we are not going to suggest an absolute figure of calories that you should be aiming for. If you are overweight you should look at food items that are low in calories and use more of these in your diet. If you are worried by the type of fat that you are eating you can look at the tables and see how to exchange one type of fat for another. The message here is to be sensible! You are more likely to stick to a change if you do not attempt to make it a drastic one.

The following tables provide an analysis of different types of food in terms of their fat content and total energy value (in calories). There is more information immediately following this list regarding the particular details in each of the tables. They are presented together for ease of reference, although you should bear in mind the comments made afterwards.

The tables are presented for ease of reference in block form. Each block length represents 100 per cent, which makes it easier to compare different tables.

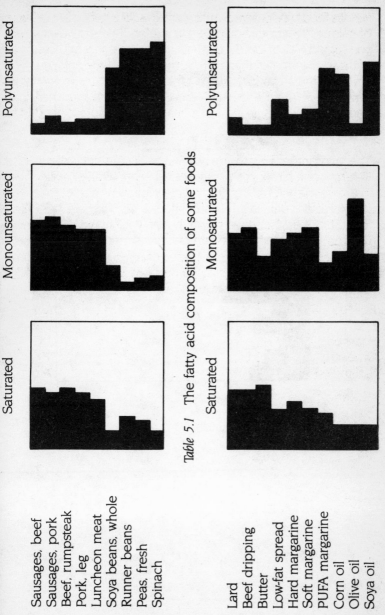

Saturated | Monounsaturated | Polyunsaturated

Sausages, beef
Sausages, pork
Beef, rumpsteak
Pork, leg
Luncheon meat
Soya beans, whole
Runner beans
Peas, fresh
Spinach

Table 5.1 The fatty acid composition of some foods

Saturated | Monosaturated | Polyunsaturated

Lard
Beef dripping
Butter
Low-fat spread
Hard margarine
Soft margarine
PUFA margarine
Corn oil
Olive oil
Soya oil

Table 5.2 The fatty acids of some fats

Table 5.3 The effect of cooking potatoes on their fat content

	% fat	Energy (kcal/100g)
Deep fried chips		565
Baked		90
Boiled		70
French fried		127
Mashed		97

Table 5.4 The effect of cooking on the fat content of eggs

	% fat	Energy (kcal/100g)
Raw, white		150
White		4
Yolk		339
Dried		564
Boiled		147
Fried		232
Poached		155
Omelette		190
Scrambled		246

Table 5.5 The effect of cooking on various meat preparations

	% fat	Energy (kcal/100g)
Beef, rumpsteak, grilled		218
Pork, leg roast		286
Sausages, beef — fried		269
Sausages, beef — grilled		265
Sausages, pork — fried		317
Sausages, pork — grilled		318
Beefburgers — fried		264
Luncheon meat		313
Sausage rolls		479
Pork pie		376

Table 5.6 Typical meals and their fat content

The bars still represent percentage fat but the portions now are not 100g but realistic quantities. The energy value is for the whole portion.

Breakfast	% fat	Energy (kcal/100g)
1 oz (30g) eggs, 1 oz (30g) grilled bacon, fried tomato, 1 large sausage, fried bread (2oz/55g)		695
Boiled egg on toast		252
2 slices of toast, butter and marmalade		620
Bowl of cornflakes, milk and sugar		145
Scrambled eggs on toast		238

Lunch

	% fat	Energy (kcal/100g)
Welsh rarebit (1 slice)		365
6 fl oz (180ml) tomato soup, bread roll and butter		319
4 oz (115g) cauliflower cheese		358
Cheese omelette (6 oz/170g)		447
1 oz (30g) cheddar cheese		117
4 oz (115g) cottage cheese		123
1 oz (30g) full cream cheese		232

Sauces

	% fat	Energy (kcal/100g)
Bread sauce (4 oz/115g)		110
Brown sauce (2 oz/55g)		48
Cheese sauce (4 oz/115g)		198
Pickle (2 oz/55g)		65
Salad cream (2 oz/55g)		150
Tomato ketchup (2 oz/55g)		48
White sauce (4 oz/115g)		151

Confectionery

		Energy (kcal/100g)
Chocolate, milk (4 oz/115g)		590
Chocolate, plain (4 oz/115g)		550
Mars bar (4 oz/115g)		441
Bounty (4 oz/115g)		473
Boiled sweets (4 oz/115g)		327
Toffees (4 oz/115g)		430

Dinner	% fat	Energy (kcal/100g)
8 oz (225g) fish (cod and batter), 10 chips, 4 oz (155g) broad beans		620
8 oz (225g) roast beef with Yorkshire pudding, 2 roast potatoes, 4 oz (115g) carrots, 1 oz (25g) cabbage		886
6 oz (170g) Cornish pastie and 10 medium chips and 4 oz (115g) carrots		726
4 oz (115g) tripe, 6 oz (170g) mashed potatoes and 4 oz (115g) carrots		306
8 oz (225g) quiche Lorraine, French bread, butter and salad dressing		1025
6 oz (170g) steak and kidney pie, 1 boiled potato and 2 oz (55g) peas		662
8 oz (225g) hot pot		258
8 oz (225g) beef stew		270
6 oz (170g) chicken leg (grilled), 8 chips and 4 oz (115g) cauliflower		258
6 oz (170g) pork chops (grilled), baked potato and 4 oz (115g) cabbage		690
8 oz (225g) white fish, 2 boiled potatoes, 4 oz (115g) peas		412

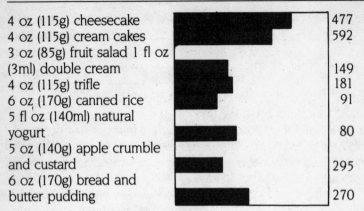

4 oz (115g) cheesecake	477
4 oz (115g) cream cakes	592
3 oz (85g) fruit salad 1 fl oz (3ml) double cream	149
4 oz (115g) trifle	181
6 oz (170g) canned rice	91
5 fl oz (140ml) natural yogurt	80
5 oz (140g) apple crumble and custard	295
6 oz (170g) bread and butter pudding	270

Notes to the Tables

Tables 1 and 2: Fatty acid compositions

The NACNE report in Britain (1984) recommended that about 30 per cent of the total energy in food should come from fat, of which only about 10 per cent should be from saturated fat. At present saturated fats provide about 18 per cent of our total calorie intake, so this means a reduction in saturated fats by about one-half. Fats high in saturated fats are typically animal in origin. You might find, for example, that cutting down on sausages and increasing vegetables in your diet will dramatically alter the amount of saturated fat that you consume. Another good way of making a change would be to consider the fats and oils that you use in cooking. Substituting soya oil for lard would be one way of shifting the balance. It is worth noting here the hard margarines contain less polyunsaturated fats than the soft margarines or polyunsaturated margarines. You obviously have to think carefully about the type of margarine that you intend to buy. The polyunsaturated margarines include those based on soya and sunflower seed oil. Table 1 contains a low-fat spread. This is often referred to as a margarine but in fact this is incorrect. By the food regulation 'margarine' may contain no more than 16 per cent water.

The low-fat spread is a highly whipped margarine and water mix which has a very high water content. It is unsuitable for cooking but can be used if you do not have the willpower to restrict your intake by other means.

Tables 3 and 4: The effect of cooking on fat content

A major contribution to the total fat in your diet comes from the fats and oils that you add when preparing and cooking the food. We have chosen two examples to illustrate this point — potatoes and eggs. The same advice could apply to any foodstuff that can be cooked in a number of ways.

A straightforward comparison of deep-fried chips and boiled potatoes shows the remarkable difference in fat content very clearly. The increased fat content of mashed potatoes comes from adding milk and butter in the mashing process.

Turning our attention to the fat content of eggs you should notice, first of all, that the egg white contains no fat — it is all in the egg yolk. All processing, apart from boiling, increases the fat content by virtue of the added fat.

The message from these tables is that reducing the fats used in cooking goes a long way to cutting down on the overall fat in your food.

Table 5: The effect of cooking and processing meat products

Sausages, luncheon meat and pork pies all have fats added in their processing. Compare the unprocessed meat with its processed counterpart. Food manufacturers are certainly becoming conscious of public opinion and are adjusting their methods in order to prepare foodstuffs containing far less fat. In the short term, these products are likely to be more expensive than the original item but it will not be long before the price gap is adjusted.

The second important factor is the way in which you cook the food. Grilling is preferable to frying in every situation.

Table 6: Typical meals and their fat content

These are, perhaps, the most important details presented in this chapter. In most circumstances you are concerned with the overall fat composition of the food and not the content of a specific foodstuff.

Some differences can be pointed out. There is an enormous difference in the fat content of a cereal breakfast and the traditional English breakfast, which also contains a high proportion of saturated fat.

What is most surprising is that most meals, such as Welsh rarebit and cheese omelette, are so high in fat. This depends on the type of cheese that is used, which is usually Cheddar. Full cream cheese contains an even higher proportion of fat. Sandwiches have been left out of this list due to the difficulties in assessing typical compositions. An important fact to bear in mind, however, is that if you choose something like cream cheese and cucumber sandwiches, you are probably eating quite a high-fat food due to the cream cheese. It is also important to consider whether you use butter or a low-fat spread in these sandwiches.

Chocolate and sweets may make interesting reading. The fat in the chocolate comes from the milk and added fats whereas boiled sweets contain no fat but still have a high energy content which comes from their high sugar content.

Main courses for dinner are the major source of nutrition for most of us and a few meals are given in total. There is a very large difference between fried fish and the same fish boiled and served with boiled potatoes. The other meals appear to have high fat contents but this should be viewed in their context as the main meal of the day.

We often like to round off a good meal with a dessert but we should be careful in our choice of sweet. Cheesecake and cream cakes should certainly be taken in moderation.

Guidelines

As we have pointed out, you have to be honest with yourself in sorting out your particular requirements. You have a lot of information now on how to balance your diet in relation to fat. If you have access to a computer you can tackle the problem systematically and objectively. There are a number of good programs available such as: *Jane Bird Master Diet Planner*, published by Silverlind for use on the Sinclair Spectrum 48K; *Microfitness*, published by VO2 for the Sinclair Spectrum 48K; *Microweight*, published by Little Softie for the Commodore 64; *Watch Your Weight*, published by Acornsoft/Which? for the BBC Micro.

Generally the programs begin by determining your 'ideal' weight, which is based on your height and other factors such as lifestyle and activity. You may then be given certain goals to aim for. If you are interested in any of the programs, first examine what you hope to get out of the program then assess if the information will be of some use to you.

For the majority of people certain guidelines should help in designing diets for health. These can be summarized in a list of Do's and Don'ts.

Do
- Keep a close watch on your total fat intake.
- Watch your total calorie intake.
- Eat low-fat foods in preference to high-fat foods.
- Grill instead of frying.
- Use a fat high in polyunsaturates instead of saturated fats.
- Trim off excess fat from meat.
- Cook meals in their own fat rather than adding extra fat.
- EAT LESS FAT.

Don't
- Eat too much.
- Fry all your food.
- Use extra fat to fry with.
- Eat fatty joints.
- Eat snacks between meals.

Finally, to help you with these recommendations here is a brief list of some common high- and low-fat foods:

Avoid	Allowed
High-fat food	Low-fat food
Butter, margarine, lard, dripping, suet pudding, vegetable oils, fried foods, mayonnaise, pastry, cream, chocolate, toffees, nuts, crisps, duck and goose.	Lean meat, chicken, turkey, cottage cheese, yogurt, skimmed milk, white fish, fruit and vegetables.

All the information you need to follow these guidelines is contained in this book, with the reasons why you should follow it. If you stick to this advice you will certainly improve your diet and you will also reduce your risk of developing such illnesses as heart disease.

Index